Angel
WINGS

POEMS OF FAITH FROM THE JOURNEY

EVELYN DAHLKE

Order this book online at www.trafford.com
or email orders@trafford.com

Most Trafford titles are also available at major online book retailers.

Printed in the United States of America.

ISBN: 978-1-4907-4295-3 (sc)
ISBN: 978-1-4907-4297-7 (hc)
ISBN: 978-1-4907-4296-0 (e)

Library of Congress Control Number: 2014913652

Trafford rev. 07/29/2014

 www.trafford.com

North America & international
toll-free: 1 888 232 4444 (USA & Canada)
fax: 812 355 4082

"Evelyn's poems are a journey

speaking to the heart."

"Evelyn's poems reveal her soul.

Her dark times draw her more

deeply into the presence of God,

and she leads the readers

into greater intimacy with themselves

and with their understanding

of the Holy One."

Contents

Foreword xi

Untitled xvii

The Early Poems...

Torn Reflections 3

Questions 4

Butterfly Song 5

Most Precious Gift 6

Alone 7

Just Hold Me 8

Time To Be 9

Hope Thought 11

Perspective On Prosperity 12

Psalm Of Hope 13

Wondrous Love 14

My Jesus 15

Easter Song 16

Spring Morning Sounds 17

The Voice Of God 18

Petition For Patience 20

Angel Wings 21

Angels Of Love 22

Contemplation 23

Most Blessed Encounter 24

Finality 25

Dark Angel 27

Sweet Parting 29

Depression's Limbo 30

Gift Of Love 31

Dark Contemplation 32

A Simple Lesson 33

Restless Uncertainty 35

Farewell 37

Poems Along The Way...

Where Are You, God? 41
Empty Spaces.. 43
Snow On A Stone-Cold Bench.. 44
Who Am I Now?.. 46
The Place of Non-Being 49
Strings Of Words 50
Peaceful Musing... 52
The Where 54
Blessing To One Who Cries 55
Easter Lily Blooming.. 56
Angel Visit 57
Silent Pondering.. 58
Scorpion.. 61
Shadows Walking... 63
River 64
Silenced Sirens 66
O, Harriet, Thou Art Holy Water....................................... 67
Mermaids Singing.. 70
Little Balloon 72
Last Farewell 74
Who Are You To Me? 75
Great Tehom 76
By Hands 77
Little Smiling Yellow Fish 79
Bell Song... 81
As The Skies Cried Gray... 83
Experience... 84
To Dare.. 87
What Color Is The Night?.. 89
Water Music... 92
Train In The Night... 94
Struggle Of Triumph 96
There To Here 97
The Sea 99
Stone From The Sea..101
Exile...103

She And I 106
Candlesticks On The Lake 108
Prairie Child 109
Prayer Without Words.. 110
Vine Prayer.. 111
Sending Psalm 112

Later Poems...

A Pastor's Doubt 117
Faltering Faith... 119
You Met Me There 120
Willow, Why Are You Weeping? 122
Begging Woman 125
The Voice 128
Home In God's Arms... 130
Pigeons On The Marquee.. 131
The Road Rose Up 132
Yet She Was My Mother.. 133
Just Yesterday 135
Rain In The Night.. 138
Spirits Rising... 139
Dancing Leaves.. 141
Season's Changing... 142
Psalm Of Joy.. 143
O God, You Are My God... 144
My Trinity 145
Busy Hands Now Still.. 147
Sunflower Time.. 148
Simple Thought... 149
Melting Snow... 150
Voice Crying In The Wilderness................................ 151
Whispering God Prayer... 153
Angels Song 155
A Dream 156
Imminent Birth.. 157
Living Bookends 158
Love Pledge.. 159

Value 161
In My Own Skin 162
The Meshing 164
Returning 166
You Carry Me 169
Happiness Crept In 171

Foreword

I've always enjoyed poetry. I think poetry, better than any other literary form, expresses feelings and emotions to the highest heights and to the deepest depths. It can take the reader from the pure happiness of a playful, rhyming sonnet to the cavernous grief of free-form, but very picturesque, verse in which the author pours out emotions crying to be let loose, to be heard.

The poetry herein shows, first and foremost, my own great faith in God in all circumstances. I've always realized that my life was in God's hands, but my faith became stronger and more notable at the time these poems began to come into being. In all, the poems reflect my personal journey with God, a reflection of where I have been and where I am now.

Secondly, I think these poems show my growth process over the twenty years in which they were written, a growth in the ability to accurately and fully translate feeling into written word in a descriptive and reflective way. Whether rhyming or free-form, they tell a story of confusion, pain, despair, and grief, followed by healing, insight, and, finally, new life, all smothered in faith. All of them put words to an interior experience to give it voice. Hopefully some will speak to you, to your own sense of wonder, or joy, or hurt, or grief—to your own recovery process, if needed. Maybe they will prompt you to experience your world more fully in a new and different, deeper way.

I'd never considered myself to be a poet. I was too busy raising children, working full time as a teacher/program coordinator for persons with disabilities, and being a helpmate on the dairy farm my husband and I owned, which took every extra moment of the day or night and then some. But that changed some twenty years ago when I suddenly found myself so full of feelings, so full of emotions, I could not help but express myself in the poetry found in this collection.

You see, twenty years ago I fell into a deep hole. The stress of abuse, torrential downpours ruining the crops on our farm, and difficulties at work came together to plummet me into a deep, dark, clinical depression. Over time, I became suicidally depressed, a condition that would plague me, even with treatment, for many years to come.

At the same time, two other things occurred. First of all, I felt called into the formal ministry of the church more strongly than ever. I had felt "called" a number of times earlier in life, but I had written that dream off in my mind, thinking it impossible for a farm wife, mother, and bread winner to take time for the four years of seminary education required of the Master of Divinity degree.

Secondly, I became more creative than I had ever been. I began painting again (I had a minor in Art from the university I had attended to earn my Bachelor of Arts degree). This time I did not paint farm buildings and house walls, but I designed and painted murals for the church I attended. I also painted on canvases, something I had also not done in the twenty years of my marriage. And I began writing, prose certainly, but also poetry, prayers, and meditations. At times the words just seemed to flow out of me as though they had been pent up somewhere for decades and needed release.

I did end up leaving my marriage and the farm, attending seminary, and serving congregations. That story is written in my memoir <u>Butterfly Song</u> (Plainview Press, 2007). But as I was shuffling through the writings I produced along the way, they seemed to tell more of my story in a different way, capturing more fully the pain, the joy, the sheer presence of God, personally, in my life in both dark and happier times.

You will note that in the early poems I refer to God with the male pronoun "he." In later poems I may use the feminine pronoun "she" or no pronoun at all, simply referring to God as God. My early experience of God in a patriarchal culture taught me that God was of the male gender. Seminary study exposed me to the feminine aspects of God found particularly in the wisdom literature, which in the original Hebrew, refers to God as the feminine "wisdom." Certainly God is inclusive of attributes of both genders, strong and good, kind and loving. That leaves only one pronoun in the English language to refer to God—"it." And "it" is much too impersonal for a God, who desires nothing less than a personal relationship with each of us. Perhaps the ancient Hebrews were correct when they inserted their God-word YHWH (Yahweh) into the text with each reference to God. Yet, this can become cumbersome, so sometimes pronouns must be used.

Although the poems reveal my walk with God over many years, God is especially present to me now in this "more senior" stage of my life. God has given me a life in which I can do ministry that interests me, I can have time to grandmother my grandchildren, and I can write as the words press to flow out of me. For the first time in my life, I am free to create at will. It is a gift and a blessing, and I am sure God's hand has been at work in bringing me to this point.

I want to thank all the people, who have influenced me and my writing, even though they may not be aware they did so. The love, support, thoughts, and good wishes of so many people have helped to strengthen me and my faith. All of my interactions with them, together with God's presence with me, have helped bring these writings from thought to written form. These poems are my heart and soul in writing. They are my "Angel Wings." I hope you are able to experience them in their fullness in order that God may come near to you in your journey also. May God bless your reading of them.

Evelyn

This book is dedicated to
The angels who have given me wings—

Dianne,
Jan, Janice, and Susan

Untitled

Walking around in my mind,
all my earthly concerns fall away.
I grow quiet,
subdued,
and distant.
Hush, my friends.
Listen and you will hear,
my thoughts are speaking.

The Early Poems...

Torn Reflections

I did not choose to fall that day,
I did not know one fell that way,
My ears listened well,
My heart opened wide,
To the pathway that led to my soul inside.

I gave it my all, the most, the best,
I could not sleep, nor could I rest,
My eyes saw the sorrow,
My heart felt the pain,
What did I lose? What did I gain?

To stand on the edge, to fall right in,
A practical person, where was my sin?
My hands felt the tremor,
My heart broke in half,
I only could cry, no longer could laugh.

To be apart from the flow of life,
No longer belonging because of the strife,
My feet walked in silence,
My heart laid out bare,
So was the torture. Why did I care?

The climb back out has been far and deep,
The pathway rocky, and ridged, and steep,
My hands grasp for sunlight,
My heart for the shore,
I know I can make it. Just love me some more.

Questions

How dark is the day if the sun is still shining?
How silent the hour if the music still plays?
Why do I gasp in the stillness when life's full of action?
Why count I the hours, the moments, the days?

Why is everyone talking when there's nothing worth hearing?
How far do I travel without moving at all?
How gray is the sunrise when the day's not worth living?
How far the climb up when deep down was the fall?

How long is the road when I know not the ending?
How fast flows the river when I drown in my tears?
How hot is the sand when my feet are so weary?
How cold is the heartache, how deep area the fears?

Why do I journey against my deciding?
Why do I stumble, and panic, and fall?
These questions for peace and for joy I am asking.
The Father in heaven can but answer them all!

Butterfly Song

You cannot catch a butterfly,
    you cannot hold it tight.
It is, by God's divine intent,
    designed for spacious flight.

You cannot place a butterfly
    in cage or box or jar.
It must, with artist's wings unfurled,
    dance blithely near or far.

You cannot mold a butterfly
    or tie it with a string.
Its wings you'll mar, its spirit crush,
    it's such a fragile thing.

A butterfly can't be a moth
    or insect dark and gray.
It must a touch of flavor sweet
    bestow upon its way.

A butterfly is meant to glint
    on leaf or bushes fair,
To brush a painter's dash of bright
    on flowers here and there.

A butterfly's a miracle
    sent from the heavens above,
Small and frail, yet free and fair,
    a gift of God's great love.

No, you cannot catch a butterfly,
    can't hold it in your hand.
It is, by God's creation wise,
    designed to be more grand.

Most Precious Gift

Blossoming flowers in sun's warm embrace,
    The storm's crashing thunder and wind on my face,
Glistening rainbows, the coo of a dove,
    What are all these but gifts of God's love?

Kind, gentle whispers, a strong hand to hold,
    An encouraging word, a warm place in the cold,
A hugging embrace or a pat on the back,
    If I have but these, what gifts do I lack?

Colorful leaves in a whirlwind of air,
    Hummingbird's dancing from sweet nectar fair,
The grace of a deer as it runs through the trees,
    How can I thank God for gifts such as these?

The cry of a baby or laugh of a friend,
    A cozy, warm fire and soft chair at day's end,
A fresh pot of coffee or cookie with chips,
    What praise can I give God from these humble lips?

The grain on the field, the tractor's loud roar,
    The sweet smell of clover, soft waves on the shore,
The white wisp of jet as it soars through the sky,
    How am I worthy of such gifts from on high?

What can I give God, what gift can I find,
    To thank God and praise God—a gift of what kind?
A gift of my heart and my soul it must be,
    The gift of "myself" which God first gave to me!

Alone

Alone—is a place of quiet,
    Senseless clatter crushed,
    Noisy gong and clanging cymbal silenced,
Stillness, precious stillness.

Alone—is a place of beauty,
    Delicate butterflies dancing,
    Swaying blades on sunlit hillsides singing,
Elegance, precious elegance.

Alone—is a place of moments,
    Horrid hurrying ended,
    Endless increments on graceful dials pulsing,
Hours, precious hours.

Alone—is a place of approval,
    Cruel laughter squelched,
    Widespread arms of hugging embraces beckoning,
Acceptance, precious acceptance.

Alone—is a place of happiness,
    Wondrous thoughts designing,
    Mystical melodies on clean, white canvas flowing,
Pleasure, precious pleasure.

But when "alone" becomes polluted,
    Fiendish fright coursing,
    Disowned dreads through terrified tears burning,
Alone—is a dark, scary place.

Just Hold Me

Hold me,
    hold me,
        hold me,
            hold me tight,
Hold me when the day's as dark as night.

Hold me when gray clouds come rumbling o'er,
    Hold me when waves crash upon my shore.

Take me, grasp me gently by the arm,
    Promise me you'll keep me safe from harm.

Cradle me securely in your care,
    That when I fear, I know you will be there.

Hold me in your heart, and soul, and mind,
    So peace and joy in simple things I find.

Just hold me,
    hold me,
        hold me,
            hold me tight,
Until I rest in God's eternal light.

Time To Be

Time,
Time to BE,
     just to BE,
I need time to BE with ME—
         right now.

Time—
     To lay back and watch elephant clouds
         drift slowly through the big, blue sky,
     To feel the breeze whisper against my cheek,
         softly… gently… quietly…

Time—
     Too watch a beetle running thither and fro,
         aimlessly, pointlessly scurrying everywhere and nowhere,
     To feel the sun surround me, hug me tight,
         warmth… glowing… peace…

Time—
     To feel giant snowflakes lightly land
         on sleeping eyelashes,
     To draw angel wings on smooth, white banks of canvas,
         freshness… cleanness… gracefulness…

Time—
     To imagine mystical, magical fairytale worlds
         where princes kiss my hand and bow,
     To dance in lace, organza gowns,
         flowing… swaying… dreaming…

Time—
    To feel the Spirit's presence surround me,
        fill me from within,
    To listen for the Father's voice inside my soul,
        stillness… silence… ECSTASY.

Time,
Time to BE,
    Just to BE,
I need time to BE with ME,
Time to just be ME—
        Right now.

Hope Thought

To "hope"
is to face the future
with expectancy
having the
faith
to have the
courage
to
just "let go" and "be"
accepting each moment
as it is given
with an unwaivering trust
in the
sufficiency
of
God's love.

Perspective On Prosperity

Prosperity is not a state of economic wealth,
property ownership,
personal rank and possession,
or outward appearances.
It cannot be bought with money or gold,
or won in an election,
with a lottery ticket, at the casino,
or through a sweepstakes.

Rather,
prosperity is a quality we come to possess
in our hearts and souls
as we live
in forgiving, loving, and compassionate relationships
one with another.
It requires a continuous investment of ourselves,
our time, and our emotions.
It comes most clearly through the sharing
of the personal pain and suffering
of the human experience.
It is a <u>gift</u> of a gracious and loving God,
who will not "give up" on us.

Come, become "prosperous" with me!
Come and <u>live</u>!

God is waiting for us!

Psalm Of Hope

God,
How I need
Your constant LOVE!

When a weak breeze of resistance
flows along my path,
the "clay vessel"
which I am
falls and shatters.
But,
You do not forsake me.

You comfort me in my brokenness.
You cradle my aching soul,
You mend my shattered heart
and
build me once again.

You send me forth—
Your messenger.

And I am able to endure
because of
Your unfaltering
and
ever-present
LOVE.

Wondrous Love

O "Wondrous Love,"
you, who hung forlornly on the tree of death—
despised,
forsaken by those of us for whom you grimly suffered,
forgotten by those of us so busy entertaining "living"
we fail to see true "life"
when it looks us deeply in the eyes.

You grasp our souls so tightly,
we gasp within the holiness of the gap
between our "living"
and the true "LIFE"
you freely offer.
We choke against the force
of your mighty power.

We bow in our unworthiness
as you pour your resurrection strength
deep within our undeserving hearts.
By your tears we are washed clean—clean to live your "LIFE,"
clean to live in you.

We rise, your servants, uplifted—
ready for the journey,
carried forth in grace by you,
O "Wondrous Love."

My Jesus

Oh, do you know my Jesus,
　　　My love, my life's delight,
　　The kind and gentle Savior,
　　　Who makes our dark world bright?

Oh, have you met my Jesus,
　　The holy Son of God,
　　　Who wraps his arms around you,
　　When rough's the path you trod?

Oh, have you learned of Jesus,
　　Who taught us how to pray,
　　　That when we cry in sorrow,
　　We'll turn the Father's way?

Oh, have you smiled with Jesus,
　　When hours are smooth and bright,
　　　When friends in care surround you,
　　And your heart in joy is light?

Oh, have you felt my Jesus,
　　So deep within your heart,
　　　Love fills you so completely,
　　You'll never from him part?

Yes, you must live for Jesus,
　　Who suffered for your soul,
　　　That sin's tight grasp would be destroyed,
　　And you would be made whole!

Easter Song

Alleluia! The Angels cry,
Glorious chorus from
The realms on High!
The Savior lives,
Death's grasp is gone,
Let your heart rejoice,
Lift your voice in song!

Alleluia! The dark day's past,
Christ is risen,
We can live at last!
The battle's over,
The stones away,
Sing Alleluia,
Joyous Easter Day!

Spring Morning Sounds

I heard the rooster crowing,
    As dawn broke the eastern sky,
Its shrill cry rang like music,
    As 'twas sent from God on high.

I heard the kittens meowing,
    From haymow cool and dark,
In cheerful romp they scuffled,
    A dance of heavenly lark.

I heard the newborn bleating,
    On bed of soft-fluffed straw,
In silky coat licked clean and smooth,
    Designed as angels draw.

I heard the cow's soft lowing,
    As morning broke to day,
Its tail swished in anxiousness,
    Its ears perked heaven's way.

I heard the buzzing bumblebee,
    Alight a dew-dropped flower,
As warmth of light and day took hold,
    God's nectar to devour.

I heard the peaceful whispers,
    Of fine butterflies in flight,
In robes of colored art arrayed,
    Which spoke of God's great might.

I heard in muted breezes,
    Of silent, tranquil rest,
My God, who walks beside me,
    A most-welcomed, loving guest.

The Voice Of God

I heard the voice of God
    in the tingling warmth of graceful breezes
        that touched against my shivering cheeks,
like fine, red sable brushing fresh, white artist's canvas.

I heard the voice of God
    in the slapping wash of welcomed waves
        that beat against the unsuspecting shore,
like steady palm-taps striking methodically smooth, unfeeling surfaces.

I heard the voice of God
    in the honking whoops of gathering geese
        that travelled V-shaped northward bound,
like regimented militants marching onward into predetermined destiny.

I heard the voice of God
    in the whimpering squeaks of baby chickadees
        that hungrily begged with jaws wide opened,
like helpless urchins crying for affluent wastes.

I heard the voice of God
    in the blissful beaming of new-risen sunshine
        that cuddled warm and pink upon my fingertips,
like burning flames baking warmth from wintery frost.

I heard the voice of God
    in the whispering flutter of butterfly wings
        that emerged victorious from ugly, death cocoons,
like carefree prisoners erupting from hellish confinements.

I heard the voice of God
    in the bursting forth of crocus petals
        that dewdrop-sprinkled forged passages of rainbow trails,
like broken splash of multi-colored inks from painter's palette.

I heard the voice of God
    in the twittering harmony of robin's singing
        that melodiously announced the rebirth of life,
like organ tunes caroling anthems of resurrected greeting.

I heard the voice of God
    in the pulsing welcoming of dawning spring
        that soundlessly transpired in the constant flow of time,
like shadows shifting incessantly on silent, ancient sundials.

I heard the voice of God
    shape life songs in tones of spring pastels
        that spoke of LOVE, and PEACE, and HOPE,
and, behold... It was very BEAUTIFUL!

Petition For Patience

Lord…
> Grant me the patience to listen
>> for voices I don't often hear.
> Help me to see into pathways,
>> when the trails seem vague and unclear.

Lord…
> Send me the patience to quietly
>> wait for the answers to come,
> to accept each new day in its freshness,
>> and attend as each task must be done.

Lord…
> Speak to me softly in silence,
>> and soothe me as kind, gentle balm.
> Help me to consciously follow
>> your example so patient and calm.

Lord…
> Lead me to see what your plan is,
>> to know why you call me in strife.
> Take me serenely and lead me,
>> that your patience and love fill my life.

Angel Wings

May God—
    Send you forth on angel wings
    That smooth your path may be,
    That as you trod along your walk
    You may God's blessings see.

May God—
    Lift your load with angel wings
    And carry you along,
    That God with you in darkest hour
    May bless your life with song.

May God—
    Walk with you, as angel wings
    Protect you on your way,
    That you might bless those you surround
    And brighten up their day.

May God—
    Grace your steps with angel wings
    And give you wisdom fair,
    That as you work or as you play
    God's love you always share.

May God—
    Raise you up on angel wings
    As eagles gently soar,
    That as you reach your journey's end
    Rest waits at Heaven's door.

Angels Of Love

I saw angels near your window,
    they were standing in your yard.
There were angels in the treetops,
    And along the boulevard.

I saw angels in your kitchen,
    One was sitting on a chair.
Some were lying on the sofa,
    And standing on the stair.

I saw angels in your bedroom,
    And even on your bed.
They were sitting on the foot end,
    And hov'ring near your head.

And then I saw God smiling,
    From not so far above,
For God had sent the angels,
    To bathe you in his love.

Contemplation

I do not know just what it was
    that came to me that day,
What'er it was, it swept me strong
    and took me far away.

Perhaps it was the trumpeting
    of lilies in full bloom,
Or maybe sun-glazed daisies
    I had placed within the room.

It could have been the glist'ning sun
    that shone on tear-dropped rain,
Or maybe just the gentle breeze
    that swept through ripened grain.

Perhaps it was the colored leaves
    that fell from painter's tray,
Or maybe frisky, foxtail stems
    that tickled on my way.

It might have been the caterpillar
    so fuzzy on the ground,
Or maybe it was joyful caws
    of blackbirds flying 'round.

What'er it was, it came to me
    a message to impart,
Because, within, the voice of God
    was written in my heart.

Most Blessed Encounter

This day I feel like crying,
    the tears are close at hand,
The air hangs still and silent
    a blanket o'er my land.

The sun's blaze, low and heavy,
    burns shadows, dark and dry,
My throat breathes parched and sullen,
    "Dear God," my soul cries, "Why?"

My knees bow down in anguish,
    my hands I clasp in prayer,
There are no words within my lips,
    but yet my Father's there.

Each tear I shed in torment,
    that trickles down my cheek,
He grasps as gold within his palm,
    a token from the meek.

Each breath I take, he fills with wealth,
    a treasure he holds dear,
He shares my deepest, darkest hour,
    and stays for me so near.

He comes, my consolation,
    my hope, my future bright,
I sense that in my gravest hour,
    He'll rescue me with might.

So in the silent stillness,
    He brings me calm retreat,
That in and by my journey,
    both Heaven and Earth can meet.

Finality

Deloris Bergs,
where are you now?

Tell me,
what was it like
that fateful day
when water's swirl
brought you to the test
and did your very life molest
to bring you to eternal rest?
Tell me,
what was it like?

Deloris Bergs, you went
through woods and meadow
to the shore.
Can I not walk
a mile more?
And, as I come
within the sight,
reach out your hand
and grasp mine tight
that I might also
come to "light"
through water's sweet deliverance.

Deloris Bergs,
if you could meet
that final test,
then let me also
come to rest.
You
went in fun.
I come shattered
and undone.

Deloris Bergs,
if you could die,
then surely,
surely,
so can I.

Dark Angel

Dark angel,
Why did you come to me?
    Just to lay your heavy yoke
    upon my shoulders
    and bring me misery?

Did I ask for you to come?
    Did I ask to be undone?
        Surely not,
        for I knew not even who you were,
        or that you even were for sure.

Did you come as friend or foe?
    This answer I do not yet know.
But this truth I know and tell.
    I've shared my space with you,
        for days, and weeks, and years as well.
My outer vestibule wasn't good enough for you.
    You chose in heart and soul to dwell.

Some say you came to me as "gift"
    in order from the depths to lift,
    my life to sift,
        grain by grain by painful grain,
        that not one hellish stain remain.

For whatever cause,
      you know you've put my life in pause.
I've had no choice,
      you make me listen to your voice,
and somewhere,
      deep within the soul
          you resonate
            to make me whole.
Somehow, buried in the strife,
          I start to breathe
            a breath of life.

Sweet Parting

For Susan

I cannot say "good bye,"
    so final is its sound.
It signifies the ending
    to a friendship I have found.

I will not say "farewell,"
    it means that we will part,
And how can I take leave of one
    I hold within my heart.

I cannot say "adieu,"
    though sweet its sound may be,
It manifests an end with one
    who means the world to me.

So I will say "God's speed,"
    in everything you do,
For when I live in heaven's realm,
    I know you'll be there too.

Depression's Limbo

Depression's limbo—
    is a place of being neither up nor down, not here nor there.
It is a suspension in "purposelessness," a reaching
    without grasping.
It sinks its pitiful victim into an emptiness that weighs so heavily,
    the lungs can barely rise against its worthless weight.

Depression's limbo—
    is a sense of "senselessness," a contradiction of the knowing.
It tastes and smells of bitter sourness which may wet the thirsty
    taste buds, but leaves a burning in the nostrils and a putrid
    rankness in the throat.
It feeds on itself, pulling incessantly deeper and deeper into
    bottomless stanch.

Depression's limbo—
    is the sound of "soundlessness," a discord of reality.
It is the simultaneous striking of adjoining, unharmonious organ
    keys.
It holds fast to unpleasant, reverberating noise until the ears ring
    garbled and the head aches dull with its throbbing lack of
    reason.

Depression's limbo—
    is a feeling of "feelinglessness" which echoes into nothingness.
It is a crumbling of humanness into a shattering of desire, a
    purgatory of the soul.
It breathes its dreary stupor in whispers of pain and death, and
    death and pain again…

    unending…
        unending…
            unending…

    this depression's limbo.

Gift Of Love

A gift of love the Father gave,
    on one fall day to me,
As in a calm repose I sank,
    within my own deep sea.

The rush was o'er, the hassle past,
    tight schedules went unkept.
I watched the rain upon the sill,
    as in my world I wept.

The voices harsh and shouting fierce,
    no longer touched my heart,
For on that day, with set of sun,
    my spirit tore apart.

In haze of death-like stormy flow,
    so tossed and turned I fell.
Like dried up leaf from tree branch torn,
    I spiraled into "Hell."

But as I floundered in the depths,
    the Father held me tight.
He soothed the hurt and wiped the tears
    and lifted me to flight.

'Twas then I saw the rainbow shine,
    and heard the angels' song,
As warmth of sun and whisp'ring breeze
    spoke "hope" from heaven's throng.

And in the silence of my night,
    God's peace I came to see,
For in my solitude so deep,
    God gave me "time" for "me."

Dark Contemplation

The road before me forked stands,
  two paths in darkness yearn.
The one leads into rocky trails,
  whose corners twist and turn.
It leads on up and down and forth,
  through dangerous, unknown gale.
And if I choose to follow it,
  I fear my strength might fail.

The other path, an abyss stands,
  from whence there's no return.
And if I cross that chasm black,
  in shadows I might burn.
Its way is brief, its pathway short,
  though end I cannot see.
It breathes a fierceness in my lungs,
  that yearns and draws in me.

Both trails I know will end in light,
  a glorious rainbow blending,
In blissful calm I'll rest in thee,
  in love that's never ending.
But yet today the road ahead
  in mystery forked stands.
Which trail I take I cannot say,
  for each brings unknown lands.

A Simple Lesson

As far as the eye can see,
the golden expanse
of the ripened grain
salutes its creator
and
bows in holy humility.
Its time is brief.
This day
it will soak up
royal beams of sunshine,
tomorrow
singing blades and whirling reels
will give it quickened rest.
It will be harvested,
and
it will fulfill its purpose.

The golden grain,
in humility, shows me,
strengthens me also
to follow the purpose
set forth for me
by my creator.
Why do I argue?
Why am I disobedient?
Why do I doubt?
Why do I fear my Father's intent?

In simple trust
I will walk my walk of faith,
knowing its purpose
has been ordained
for me
before the beginning of time.
Can I not take a simple lesson
from the grain
of the field?

Restless Uncertainty

There is a "restless uncertainty"
on this day—"the day before."
I'm not sure
words can even do justice
to the feeling of gaping chasm
deep within my chest.
For today is a day of dying—
a dying to the past, the usual,
the customary, the routine.
And in the dying of today, there is a silent screaming
that refuses to allow me to work.
The constant motion
of my body doing nothing
tires me.
And my fingers pulse
with incessant, useless energy.
The screaming within cries in tones
of fear and awe,
wonder and nervous overwhelmment.
And I can hardly contain myself.

I watch the silent ripple
of peaceful waves
contentedly held
on water's buoyant surface,
glowing with white-golden tranquility,
safely held
in the eternity of their holy creation.

God,
Why do I not feel so safely cradled?
Or, in my anxiety
am I pushing you away?

A tear is spent
in terrorizing uncertainty.
One calming tear.

Bless me with your peace, Lord
today, in this day of dying,
for tomorrow
I begin to be reborn.

Farewell

To bid one last farewell,
    I walked around the farm,
How peacefully it breathed on me,
    a breath that brought me harm.

Aged grasses cracked beneath my feet,
    dried leaves rustled in the breeze,
Ripened crops stood patiently
    for readied combine's wheeze.

The howl of tractor's roar,
    wagons bumping on the way,
Carried harvest sounds in dark'ning night
    that held familiar sway.

The crispness of the night,
    its cool brush upon my face,
The scents of nature's woodedness
    enclosed me in this place.

But way up in the sky,
    among a galaxy of star,
The blinking lights and silent pass
    of jet were much too far.

The glow of cities' lights,
    that beamed in eastern sky,
Reminded me the chrysalis
    must take to wing and fly.

So in the bidding of farewell,
    the tears that screamed to be,
In grief-filled spaces also spoke
    in cries to set me free.

Poems Along The Way...

Where Are You, God?

Where are you, God?
Are you here, or are you there?

God—
    Are you in the booming organ
    bellowing tunes of praise or soothing songs
    on ears of penitent, world-worn souls?
    or…
    Are you in Christ's crucifix
    hanging painfully, silently at chapel's front,
    speaking ugliness and wonder altogether
    in one breath?

God—
    Are you in the snakes of traffic
    slithering in criss-cross mazes,
    carrying work-weary faces homeward
    as minutes rush along on well-kept hours of hurry?
    or…
    Are you at the busy traffic light
    where impatient, intolerant horns scream protest
    to dawdling pedestrians who carry packages of worldly gods
    back home to suburbia's slumber?

God—
    Are you in the eloquent melody
    of violin and bass, cello and string
    of symphony's sweet song of perfunctory praise?
    or…
    Are you on the silent hillside of fluttering grass,
    swishing and swaying to breeze's beckoning,
    where sun-warmed rays bake hopeful messages of peace
    to tired minds and aching hearts?

God—

    Are you in callused hands
    resting wearily atop weathered canes
    steadying old men's faces whose expressions bear lament
    of last night's park bench peril?
    or…
    Are you amid the chuckling, dirty smiles of street-wise kids
    romping heartily along garbage-filth trains
    of brick tenement buildings
    on trails of cement and tar?

God—

    Are you between stretched out palms
    clenched together in peaceful prayers
    with promising praises from parched lips
    and eyelids closed to worldly wonders?
    or…
    Are you planted deep within those lives
    so greatly in need of love and joy,
    reason and purpose, focus and future, hope and peace
    that your strength becomes their strength
    and your presence cannot be denied?

God, where are you?
Are you here, or are you there?

I thank you that you're everywhere!

Empty Spaces

In my spaces dark and deep,
that is where I vigil keep,
in those silent, empty spaces,
in the dark and dreary places,
there
I reach for breaking light
when glimpses are but fading sight,
to place my feet on solid ground
when rock or soil cannot be found,
there
to hold with strength secure
when grasp for meaning rests unsure,
to smell and taste a tranquil rest
while soul and spirit cry unblessed

In those silent, empty spaces,
in the dark and dreary places,
in the sea of no relief,
that is where I cry in grief,
to grow,
to know,
to learn, to find
what may in empty spaces hide.

There is where I vigil keep,
in those spaces, dark and deep.

Snow On A Stone-Cold Bench

The snow on the stone-cold bench
rests quietly in its curled clump,
glazed and crystallized,
icy cold,
silenced on the shady side of sun,
which cannot reach to cuddle with its warmth
… leaving only room for one to stay and chat
her lonely story of remembering red roses
resting in green basin,
tinged by frosty February gusts
twenty-five years in passing
… the smell of rotting roses
in the room of her existence,
now laid to rest, dried and curled,
in gentle tissues of cardboard coffin,
buried tenderly
in a memory that cradles eternity
in all her empty spaces.

The years from there to here
are but heart-shaped cookies
left uneaten,
sleeping on a paper plate,
sprinkled with her reddened tears
and framed by painful edges,
yet blessed with pink-frosted babes
… years, stretching from thirteen to thirteen,
across the expanse of lifetime,
beyond the timepiece's face.

Yet the clock ticks,
but now of gentle pulses of the river
and of the "foreverness" of peaceful slumber.

The bench is cold and lonely,
one-sided, "alone," and still,
so,
celebrate this Valentine's without me,
for the journey only leads "away."

Who Am I Now?

The lawyer spoke
    as we exited the courtroom door.
His words rang deep:
    "You've been single now four-and-a-half minutes.
    How does it feel?"
I looked at him, but there was no answer.
    How does one give answer
    to what one does not herself understand?
And, who am I now?

I have left behind those traditional descriptions
    of who I am-the "wife," the "teacher,"
      the "program coordinator," the "youth leader,"
      the "present parent"—
    and I am a stranger in the very land
      that gave me roots,
    now connected only by "motherhood" and
      memories that tug at heartbeats
        and play like an incessant video
        in private recesses of my mind,
      like intimate unreality.
And often I am haunted by my knowing incapacity
    to be that which I am becoming.
So then, who am I now?

I live a stranger in a foreign land,
    and to be "single" or "married"
      at this point seems immaterial,
    for neither term holds meaning
      for one who does not even know herself.
I feel the emptiness of an immigrant,
    who tries hard not to give away
      the secret of her own ignorance,
or like I'm performing a role in a play,

a role for which I never auditioned.
I roll along the freeways,
    I walk among the skyscrapers, I pass before the Capital,
        cathedrals, and universities as if they somehow
        belong to me.
I live next to lions and tigers and Japanese gardens,
    I watch jet liners take off to foreign lands
        and return again just above my head
        as if such a sight was just a part of any ordinary day.
These things are no longer something
    momentarily visited or imagined from a distance,
        no longer a picture I see on television.
I feel like a Titanic survivor,
    floating precariously in a lifeboat,
        visioning from a distance the spectacle
        of a former reality sinking ever more quickly
        into a sea of unreality.
So then, who am I now?

It has been nearly five years now since I, like Paul,
    met God on the road to Damascus.
Still yet, I question, "Who am I now?"
    Single, alone, and lonely,
        yet, a mother, a student, an intern,
        a soon-to-be "pastor,"
    living in a world in which I never could have imagined
        I would be,
    in a life filled with new horizons, new relationships,
        new experiences, new pathways to be followed.
Who am I now as I wander this maze of wilderness,
    of new unknowingness,
  as I continue to sail to Ninevah
    when Tarshish seems the wiser, "kinder" choice?

I am the one who still walks a trail of trust
    that I yet do not understand,
  the one who continues to listen to a voice
    that I am unworthy of hearing.
I am the one who is led by a Spirit
    beyond my imagining,
  who experiences a forgiving
    beyond my deserving.
I am the one who has relinquished the future
    to a God who will not give up on me.

O, how God (still) walks with me!

The Place of Non-Being

Have you ever been to the place of non-being—
    a place where thinking and feeling
    are hung in suspension and
        mesh into nothingness altogether?

It is a place of total disconnection,
    a place separate from day-to-day reality,
    a faraway place where one retreats
        when human relationship fails to keep its grasp
        on a soul that's yearning to escape.

This place is so deeply embedded in one's thought
    that its endless river flows into an eternity
        where sparkles of sunrays glimmer;
        where all that _is_
        fades into a muted, multi-colored backdrop
            to the scene of a drama
            that one no longer acts upon,
                a game board from which
                one withdraws its playing piece.

It is a pleasant place because pain has stayed behind.
    the bodily senses no longer feel the separation,
    and the abandonment
        no longer drives its sworded knife into the soul.

I know the way to the place of non-being.
    the trail is mapped into the recesses of my mind
        where neuron meets neuron
            in an uncanny pattern of remarkable capability
            butted up against extreme non-desire
            of present reality.
It is the place where the "Pearl of Great Price" resides.

Perhaps someday you will join me there.

Strings Of Words

Strings of words,
    left unsaid, unheard,
    mingled into whimpering tones,
    twisted deep in bloody intestines
      where melodies
        of unworded thoughts
          can't be deciphered,
            in silent abyss
            of unmapped darkness.

Strings of words,
    Strings and strings of words,
      like kite tails
        snarled far
        in aged and wounded tree branches,
          distorted, muted, weathered,
          frayed, and faded,
          kite tails of words
            silenced in wintry wind gusts
            of despair.

Strings of words,
    Strings and strings and strings of words,
      embedded into miles
      of smooth, uncracked, uncreviced highways,
        tombs of pressed-black pavement,
        tangled labyrinths
      of contorted, unvoiced stories
          leading into silenced, unkept
          nowherelands.

Strings of words,
    Strings, and strings of unvoiced words,
        unknitted, unstoried,
            untold, unheard,
                shut off, kept out,
                    floating in their sea of tears,
                    caught between the soul and mind,
                    lung and tongue—
                        these words!

Can you—
    Will you give ear to hear,
        to free them from entombed
        and silenced
            tyranny?

Peaceful Musing

You there, just beyond the graveyard's corner,
   facing west instead of east,
   who in shame-filled place have eternal lease,
      beyond the hedge of evergreen
      separating your "evil" dust
      from the "pious trust,"
   the dammed, but honest, despairing
      from those who either pretended
         to live without grief or pain,
         or were far too ignorant for caring.

You, who, unnamed, rest in wearied grasses
   beyond the bounds of caretaker's passes,
      where wildflowers dot the waving glades
      with yellow-white among swaying blades,
         sweet-singing in the prairie breeze,
         unadorned by plastic, store-bought vases,
         just flowers dancing as they please,

You, who rest unencumbered by the multitude
   of hideous mourners' parades,
   tramping neat-rowed graves
      of "nicer" folk now gone,
         who wore their smile
         to hide their guile,
      now resting in royal robe aligned,
      in formal, choral gown consigned,
         who groan in their eternal drones
         in deceitful voice of monotonous tones,

You, who crossed the great divide
                in your own moment,
            on your own time,
                in your own way,
            by your own hand sublime,
Let me to your private place come near.
It's your untold story I crave to hear,
        the uncommon, unnothingness
            by which you came to lie
                in grave remote
            from those deemed "civilized,"
        the unlistened-to legend
            judged too evil, beyond grace.
Let me come lie with you
            in your peaceful, heavenly place.

The Where

Where fog encircles the earth so tight,
　　that from ground to sky there is no light,
Where blanket of cloud covers the day
　　and sprinkles its tears in whatever the way…
　　That's where I stay!

Where burning fire scorches the ground,
　　and death calls cunningly all around,
where empty streets in circles run,
　　and evil cackles its senseless fun…
　　It's there I'm undone!

Where waters flood the mountains of earth,
　　and rivers scream murder instead of rebirth,
Where bridges collapse all tangled in haze,
　　and fences rise up in puzzling maze…
　　There are my days!

Where bloody hands reach 'neath my chin,
　　and ice on the water grows weakenly thin,
Where thunderous growls emit from the sky,
　　and gnarling fingers hold tendriling tie…
　　That's where I die!

Blessing To One Who Cries

May God rock you in her cradle,
enfold you in her arm,
as she shields you in the tempest,
keeps you safe from every harm.

May God touch your tears most precious,
collect them in her palm,
or wipe them with the cloud dust
singing lullaby of psalm.

May God bring you to her bosom,
let you nourish at her breast,
in the comfort of her heartbeat,
may you cuddle, welcomed guest.

May God brush your cheek most gently
and stroke your silky hair,
as she breathes in you her whispers
assuring of her care.

May God rock you in her cradle,
may you nap in tender fold,
as she lifts you from the darkness,
within her precious hold.

Easter Lily Blooming

There's an Easter Lily blooming
    in the safety of a cove.
Among the summer flowers,
    what a beauty to behold!

It stands up tall and proudly
    among the pinks and reds
of pansies and petunias
    blooming brightly in their beds.

Before it lie wild violets,
    sleeping low upon the ground.
and just beside its purity,
    the daisies gather round.

Behind it bright, orange lilies
    stand ready for the day,
when they will open widely
    and boldly have their say.

So perfect are its petals,
    so waxy without flaw.
among the golden marigolds,
    I simply stand in awe!

In the heat of summer sunshine,
    far beyond the spring's fresh dew,
stands the purest, whitest lily,
    God's gift to me and you.

Angel Visit

The angels must have visited
    in the darkness of the night,
For when I woke this morning,
    my world was sprinkled white.

The branches, how they glistened
    with their marv'lous, brilliant hue,
While fall blooms all lie withered,
    quick frozen in their dew.

The snow dust rushed in patterns
    as I pathed my way from home,
And I left footprints on the byway
    in whatever way I roamed.

The angel wisps, they sparkled,
    as they scattered in the breeze,
For the sun filled them with energy
    to flitter where they pleased.

The tiny flakes shone golden white,
    brushed pink and blue the air,
In crystals, diamond-like, they lit,
    a rainbow 'pon my hair.

As the sunshine rose up brighter,
    and clouds drifted on in kind,
The angels floated heavenward,
    but this "gift" they left behind.

Silent Pondering

Sky and earth are cloaked
in darkest robe of midnight black;
while, in restless lack
of sleep,
I vigil keep
waiting for spirits of night to attack.

I claim earth-hewn chair,
laid bare
on steep of river's bank;
cold and frozen, brown and dank.
It's here I'm bound by chains in flank.

Distant silhouettes send smoky drifts
of unnatural luminescence
through foggy whiffs
of nighttime mists.
The winged glow of angels gently lifts
the drench of sand that in me sifts
immortal grains revealing gifts
that mourn with water's passing.

Iron frames, clad in cement,
across expanse of river bent,
join there to here,
civility to untamed sphere
of river's flow,
which onward travels, long and low
through ticking hours of endless night,
relentlessly moving so far from sight,
yet taking a pause ever so slight,
then ruffling past,
and sliding and rushing swift to the last
of maze-like course to man-made falls,

which sends a message in whispering calls
to a listening ear
that purely can hear
a beckoning of spirit, "Come here and draw near,"
while silently grasping with tendrils aglow;
the yearning cries softly for relentless near flow.

A faint, beaming lamp post nearby serves as host,
giving a whisper of illusory boast
by sending purest candlelight
'pon liquid mirror of fluid white,
and turning night
to radiance bright,
bearing beams of glorious might
in laughing tones of true delight
through thick of air
while rays reach up, from here to there;
like spindling, probing fingers that bear
majestic chorus bent to attack
the light that I lack,
of the glow that darkness begs to hide
bearing water's expanse to river's far side.

No flowers here, nor grass of green
to form a carpet on which to lean;
no fragrant clover, daisies bright
nor rain's jubilant dancing of holy delight
to sway the attack of the dark of night;
just the sight
of the river
as it flows in its might.

And though I am here,
I fear
that I dwell far away,
where river's flow to balmy bay
bears dreams resplendent
that remarkably stay
in treasured places of mind's fretful way;
where, in time eternal, Gilead sleeps in bright array,
while so silently keeps
the hearts of the souls who long for the deeps
in search of the day.

May I take the hand
which reaches for mine,
pulling me surely over the line
that separates darkness from a light most divine?
Or must I just view the star of the light
joining the heavens to the fluid of might,
which touches me softly with radiance white,
and bears me along on its wings
as it sings
in the night?

Scorpion

O great, black scorpion of guilt,
in gruesome web you engulf my being.
You wrap your hideous tendrils
around my lungs,
and press your heavy dirge upon my throat.
In terror, I gasp for air
as your poisonous sting of venom
pierces my heart.
I feel its painful coursing,
its stinging in my fingertips and toes,
and hear in tones of death songs
memoirs of my woes.

I am cocooned in wretched loneliness
while creeping maggots
destroy my roots, eating flesh alive.
My nostrils reach for living breath,
but moldered stanch is all I smell.
My own decay.
In "lightless" day
I am undone by my own evilness,
judged condemnable,
indicted by this,
the living death of putrid, rancid guilt.

And who am I to testify
on my own behalf?
Before I speak
I stand accused by conscience.
O great, black scorpion,
this I find.
Your nest is in my mind.
And I,
engulfed in wretched, self-owned filthiness,
fall victim of your snare.
Why should I care?

I slowly drown in toxins
of your black and monstrous sea.
O scorpion, devour quick.
The pain's too thick,
The cries too deep.
Please let me lie in "lifeless" sleep.

O wretched scorpion of guilt!
O woeful worthlessness of me!

Shadows Walking

There are shadow walking—
    indifferent, transparent shadows
that flitter like misty clouds
    among crowded people
        tramping busy sidewalks,
        gathering "treasures" in their clumsy arms.

There are shadows walking—
    sneaky, slinking shadows
that creep like snakes
    between trees and trails,
    crawling craftily around lamp posts,
    molding themselves
        over slumbering beds of pansied petals,
            humming faintly-flowing melodies
            on sleepy afternoons.

There are shadows walking—
    angry, ominous shadows
that lurk like monstrous storm clouds
        over unsuspecting characters
            caught up in frivolous frenzy
            in mighty malls of irreverent aisles,
that roar in silenced rumble
        waiting for their time of hearing.

There are shadows walking—
    weeping, wandering shadows
that touch the sidewalk's surface
and ooze into pearly puddles
        beneath unsuspecting soles,
        watching, sighing shadows
that wait to be inked into reality,
    to be sentenced into existence.

Am I the only one to story them to life?

River

Silent billows on the river,
       cirrus whispers, cloudy sea,
   ceaseless patterns strangely fluent
         speak a magic artistry.

Icy wavelets sprightly dancing,
       passing icicles of grass,
   'long channel's coated ridges,
         cotton-powdered, edged with glass.

Sun-streaked prisms, diamond studded,
       scattered randomly in cold,
   tell the pattern of a story
         crying loudly to be told.

Crystal bed so neatly sleeping
       in the satin-mirrored bay,
   sparkling fables in the sunlight,
         weaving tales in the day.

Rushing fall of lace unwinding,
       stretching 'cross expanse of time,
    roaring cries of ceaseless beck'ning
        in a melody sublime.

Designer's marvel, blessed moment,
       endless passage, glorious choice,
    I search the wonder of your silence
        that bespeaks a holy voice.

Can I not reach out to join you,
       as my breath your anthem cries,
    so in the beauty of your mystery,
        I might wing your glorious skies.

Let me nod as freedom calls me;
       restless, anguished may I go,
    to write the chapters of forever
        in the peace of river's flow.

Silenced Sirens

Sirens sounding,
 Blasting, blazing,
  Whirling glow
   Of lights of red,

Yellow flashing,
 Brilliance dancing,
  Telling wave
   Of inner dread,

Evil strutting,
 Pounding, prancing,
  Laughing, showing
   No remorse,

Squad cars dashing,
 Weaving, turning,
  Inner mind,
   A raceway course,

Heart a'thumping,
 Silent-shrieking,
  Hurting pangs,
   No crying sound,

Silenced sirens,
 No one hearing,
  Stabbing wound
   In spirit bound.

O, Harriet, Thou Art Holy Water

Harriet—A nearby lake

Voices and bodies flow
on busy, man-made paths
of circularity,
coming from and going to,
beginning and ending
in both place of start and finish.

Buggies and carriages,
tee-shirts and rollerblades,
walk-men and jogging shoes,
why go you round and round
to nowhere?

Can I but break through
your monotonous trail
and descend the steep slope
to heathen ground
which human perfection has not tamed,
to soil formed
by God's own hand alone,
to crusty, rough, and rocky shore,
through seed-crowned grasses
dotted with purples, whites, and yellows
of June-toned painted artistry,
growing uninvited
and unnoticed
by the very eyes
created to crown them in eternal glory.

In private carnival of solitude
I kneel
before a pool of glowing wonder
which crosses the expanse of time,
hiding sun in shadows of indifference.

I dip my cup-shaped palm,
breaking mirrored surface
into spreading ripples,
distorting crystal images,
shattering the pane
dividing an eternity and mortality
of which I belong to both,
and yet, not either.

I contemplate the entering,
of pushing beck'ning door wide open,
escaping death-like tomb of life.

Or
is this fluid handful,
so fresh of smell and cool of touch,
God's own holy water,
spreading tides of baptismal promise
into bloody stank
of morbid chalice
I choose not now to drink from?

Amid the roar of soaring jet
I hear your voice again, O God.
I listen yet to song so sweet
and breathe of freshness,
sweet relief.

Surely, this is most holy water,
your temple,
not
my tomb.

Mermaids Singing

I can hear the mermaids singing,
    there's a chorus loud and clear,
A melody most marv'lous
    comes a-ringing in my ear.
A song of untold legend,
    and a ballad long and bold,
A whisper in the sea crest
    like a chant from lips of old.

I can feel in sea's soft swishing,
    and its lap upon the shore,
The murmur of the heartbeats
    of the mermaids on the moor.
A slow and steady pulsing,
    or a dancing, rhythmic beat,
A long, melodious flowing,
    like a field of rustling wheat.

I can see in lustrous wonder
    of the sun's ripe, golden ray,
The outline of a splendor
    in the orange at end of day.
An element of mystery
    in a shadow dark and deep,
A silhouette of elegance
    in a bold, but graceful, sweep.

I can touch in sea's soft breezes
        of a velvet smooth and clean,
A royal cape most saintly
        worn rightly by a queen.
A graceful drape flows softly,
        and deep within its fold,
The mermaids rest most holy
        on a robe of precious gold.

I can smell from salty waters
        a fragrance slowly lift.
Like a multitude of springtime flowers,
        the mermaids waft adrift.
In choruses of pearly green
        and multi-colored swirl,
The scents of wispy clouds transpire,
        a smell of angels' twirl.

I can taste in crispy wind gusts
        the sweetness of the breath
Of the mermaids' gentle moth'ring
        that lifts the soul from death.
In the taste, the touch, and smelling,
        in the feeling of sea's dew,
I can hear the mermaids singing.
        Perhaps you can hear them too.

Little Balloon

Little balloon above the treetops,
    tiny balloon so far from sight,
So fragile in the vastness,
    within the clouds you light.
Amidst the puffy billows,
    the cotton balls up high,
You float, and drift, and wander,
    in the greatness of the sky.

Do you soar and dance up yonder,
    little princess, on the breeze,
Or do you shrivel in your lostness,
    in a whimper do you wheeze?
Do you shout in great blue chasm,
    or do you scream in bloody tone,
Do you whisper in a silence,
    little balloon so far from home?

Are you crisp, and firm, and shiny,
    are you red, bright pink, or green?
Or are you black and lonely,
    transparent, clear, unseen?
Do you bear a certain majesty,
    like a queen with purple cloak,
Or is your charm most simple,
    little balloon of common folk?

Do you know the many answers,
   to the questions in your life,
Or are you torn asunder
   by the struggle, in the strife?
Do your problems gather ceaselessly,
   like weights upon your crown,
Do they pull and tug your heartbeats,
   little balloon, to bring you down?

Little balloon amid the towers,
   tiny balloon in unknown space,
You, who travel in a whisper,
   and yet ride the path of grace,
You know not where you're going,
   yet, you hear God's voice so soft,
And in the portals of God's majesty,
   you float in tender loft.

Last Farewell
Tribute to Maggie

One lone gull in splendor glides
    among the sea and sky,
In radiant splendor, glowing white,
    she dances up on high.

She floats in graceful mystery,
    around, and past, and o'er,
'bove sea of glass, a mirror blue,
    as free as gulls can soar.

Others swarm and scramble near,
    a grayish, hungry brood.
But she above wings melody,
    in tones of heavenly mood.

The sun in brightness streams the sky,
    in stroking prisms paints,
Her wings aflame, her feathers afire,
    with rainbows of the saints.

She dances o'er the rocky coast,
    and circles the silky sand,
She swirls to say one last farewell,
    to the silhouette on land.

The shadow dark against the sun,
    who knows her story true,
With tear-streaked cheeks blows tender kiss,
    to bid her farewell, too.

Then soaring upward, turning back,
    toward heaven, she spreads her wings,
And, in the silence of her flight,
    the song of angels sings.

Who Are You To Me?

For Dianne

Who are you—to me,
    As I trudge through dark of sea?
Not the fuschia rose so fair,
    Nor magenta angel hair.

Perhaps you're footprints in the sand,
    That carry me to safe of land.
Perhaps you're hand for me to grasp,
    Through dark and lonely, hurting past.

Perhaps you're bridge to help me cross,
    A wild torrent of deep-felt loss.
Perhaps you are the greenstone firm,
    That holds me up so I may turn.

Perhaps you are the tan and brown,
    That cares and smiles amid my "down."
Perhaps you're sweetest candlelight,
    That shines a ray of distant sight.

Whoe'er you are, you are a gift,
    That I am carried through this rift.
You are a gift God gave to me,
    That I might cross this darkest sea.

Great Tehom

Tehom: Hebrew word for "deep darkness," "pit"

Great wall of Tehom, so thick and so cold,
suspended from heaven, draped heavy in fold,
in smoky unknowing of wave upon wave,
enticing, entrapping me dark in your cave.

With the clamp of your empty, and your black without light,
you lure me and call me like a voice in the night.
The wailing of clouds, scattered tears in the mire,
in quiet aloneness my soul burns afire.

I stare at the canvas of your blank on the wall,
a blizzardy nothing of empty befall.
I search in the chasm for soothe to my ache,
while you pull and you tug for my footsteps to take.

I can't understand it, my mind cannot know,
the secret you hold you're so desperate to show.
I reach out my hand to a whisper unnamed,
for my mind seeks a presence and my heart yearns for flame.

In trembling unsureness with left foot, then right,
I step into your nothingness hoping there to find sight.
great wall of Tehom, so deep and so cold,
in unveiling of silence my life you take hold.

By Hands

By hands, with clay,
    I came to take form,
        primordally sculptured,
            for relationship born,
    One with creator
        of sun, stars, and morn.

By hands of divinity,
    I was woven and knitted,
        in womb of complexity
            artistically fitted,
    And in pause of a moment
        to earth was admitted.

By hands of humanity,
    so was I neglected,
        the babe of the womb
            by own mother rejected,
    No cradling arms
        to keep me connected.

By hands of a tyrant,
    I was broken and bruised,
        in mind and in spirit
            I was owned and abused,
    Raped of myself,
        both rejected and used.

By hands of concern,
    I was grasped when I'd torn,
        with firm skillful fingers
            I was given new form,
    In loving acceptance,
        with a tear, was reborn.

By hands I was woven,
    neglected, and beat,
        thumbprints in memory
           I'd like to delete.
But only **by hands**
    can "life" I regret.

So lend me your **hands**
    as I grasp in the night.
        By the skill of your **hands**
           may I find strength to fight,
That I may, with time,
    by my hands delight.

Little Smiling Yellow Fish

Little, smiling, yellow fish
    in your fairy-sea of glass,
I wonder at your majesty,
    I marvel at your class.

Although you're just a little fish
    who swims a manmade sea,
if I could hold you in my hand,
    I'd bring you home with me.

You've made your home behind a rock
    all decked in corral bright,
from where you rule in mightiness,
    from which you radiate light.

Your loyal subjects float about,
    striped, orange, and royal blue,
but in the grandeur of their flash,
    they can't compare to you.

You swim, a little sunshine,
    a coin tipped on its side,
and with a graceful swish of fin
    through fluid country glide.

You whirl about and up and through
    the fairy-sea you reign,
you catch sweet morsel, quickly turn,
    your castle to regain.

But as you pass 'long water's edge
    and dash near glassy pane,
you smile at me your "merriness,"
    and, touched, I'm not the same.

I'd like to join your fluid land,
    I, too, your subject be,
in safety of your box of home,
    humanity I'd flee.

I'd like to breathe the water fresh,
    to romp 'mong corral glade,
to swish, and curve, and float along,
    no longer be afraid.

I'd like to live in home so fair,
    to have you as my queen,
that I might learn to glide about,
    and from your wisdom glean.

But I must sit outside the glass
    to watch you from afar,
and wonder, little smiling fish,
    at the yellow that you are.

Bell Song

A bell is softly chiming,
  singing melody to me.
In gentle tunes most splendid,
  it lures me to the sea.
    It rings its tone most sadly,
      pouring tears with every stroke,
    a waterfall of memories
      cascading from its cloak.

A bell is softly calling.
  Its music fills my mind
with a symphony most marv'lous
  of another place and kind.
    The tales it pours are living
      like the breath of river's flow,
    so silently, so peacefully,
      to a place I need to go.

A bell is softly luring
  my restless soul from sleep,
while ripples on the river
  their steady glimmer keep.
    A portrait dim and murky
      with a luminescent shine
    shows the passage of a spirit
      to another place and time.

A bell is softly speaking
    in a most alluring tone
to a soul that cries incessantly,
    so tired, so lost, alone.
        I listen to its ringing,
            knowing time is on its side,
        for my spirit's leapt the barrier
            and flowed on with the tide.

A bell is softly whisp'ring.
    Its voice within my heart
speaks anxiously in characters
    where each one has a part.
        The scenes are ever playing
            from beginning to their end,
        and I know I'll lose the battle
            before their voices blend.

As The Skies Cried Gray

The skies cried gray
on the angry river
that flowed at the port,
as though it were sport
to pass the day
in a tormented way.
And so I stood
letting tears from the sky
flood over me
like I was anchored at bay,
unable to enter
yet, unable to stay
on this land side of life
ripped open with strife.
One step to the side
could have finished indeed
this endless struggle,
this lonely need
to say good-bye
and in an instant be freed
by the flow of the current,
the rush as it passed.
Unable to move
I stayed 'til the last
wet dripping caressed me,
holding me fast.
Tied to the moorage
and locked to the bay,
I wept right along
with the song of the day
as the skies cried gray.

Experience

On that day I was taken up.
As I ascended, I noted I was riding
    in a golden-winged chariot.
It had no driver and was not pulled by any power,
    but rather, was directed on its own.
As the countryside passed below me,
    I had no fear—just wonderment.
And as I gazed on it with open eyes,
    the world below me was unveiled
        as being consumed
        by petty, selfish, worthless nothingness.

My gaze turned
    as I felt a warm, firm grasp leading me.
Not moving my feet, yet I followed, as if by instinct,
    in certain familiarity.
I felt suspended, by no burdensome weight
    or cumbersome infirmity held back.

Soon I sensed a halting,
    and the firm grasp ceased to be.
Not looking with my eyes, but with my heart,
    I beheld before me the throne of God,
    God's almighty being there attending.
I "saw" God,
    the one image was of an aged, yet ageless, grandfather,
    white-bearded, smiling tenderly.
    He beckoned me come close.
Yet, as I did, I looked directly into God's eyes.
    They were the loving eyes of a grandmother,
    looking into and knowing me deeply,
    her child, her offspring,
    somehow forever connected
    by a mysterious umbilical cord of caring.

God beckoned me to come sit in her soft and cuddly lap.
At the same time, God's entire being was engulfed
    in brilliant light,
    and I was drawn forward by sheer attraction
    as I did not move my feet,
    for there was no ground to stand on.

Great and mighty, yet, gently loving hands
    cupped me at the chin.
When my forehead touched God's majesty,
    the tears upon my cheek
    appeared as tears on the face of God.
And the ache I carried beat painfully among us.
God gently planted a kiss upon my forehead;
    I felt a burning in my chest.
Then graciously the hold was released,
and God nudged me on my way.

The familiar grasp again took me by the hand.
As I turned, there stood many whom I recognized,
    though I don't know how—
        Abraham and Moses, Sarah and Miriam,
        Samuel, Deborah, Elijah, Elizabeth, John,
        Anna, Stephen, Mary Magdaline,
        and among them, Mother Mary kneeling.
At the last was Paul.
    I quivered at the knowing of him.
    On his chest was the glowing of a cross.
    It was emblazoned on his being.
On the seeing of it, so also, my chest burned.
    I grasp the burning with my palm and dared to look.
    That same cross also glowed in me.
    Fear gripped me.
Sensing this, Paul nodded peace to me.

As I took a breath, the chariot was gone,
    the images are now but memory.
But the world around me is different now, somehow empty, void.
And the cross-
    the cross is burning in my chest.

To Dare

Can I dare to look up,
to raise my gaze,
to look you straightly in the face
and know you will not laugh
or turn away,
but that your eyes
will with me stay,
so I, in them,
may see you through
the faceted cuts
to the "who' that is you
deep beyond sight,
to the soul
of your "whole"
from which there sings light?

And in their reflection,
their mirrors of glass,
can I dare to see me
with a sight that I lack?
That, in the looking through you,
I can see myself back,
not transparent or clear,
but real and here,
and so presently near.

Can I reach out my hand
and trust you to guide me
to safety of land,
that your prints mine match,
that there they attach
as mine rise in your palm,
in your hand, take their form,
their character of circles
in yours not be torn,
that, in the hold of your hand,
myself I may find
moment by moment,
like kind with like kind?

Dare I to trust you
to hold me securely,
to treat me demurely?
Can I dare,
Do I dare,
in you to trust?

What Color Is The Night?

What color is the night?
Is the night black, as black can be,
so thick with dark I cannot see
my hand before my heart?
Is it so black with emptiness
that there's no hope that morn will ever come,
that I might never see the sun
shining on a desperate soul?
Has the spill of black oozed into every cell so thoroughly
that vacuoles permeate black to black,
exchanging messages of death attack
from which there's no redeeming?
Is the night as black can be?

Or is the night so midnight blue,
it's sighing deep with melancholy,
drowned in ceaseless crying,
the lowest chasm of river's flow.
Is night blue-aching of the soul
that knows not its redeeming,
wall to wall expanse which deep in ocean lies,
no breath of air, no living sighs,
no cause to care,
just deep, dark blue from here to there,
in all ways midnight blue
as deep as one can know,
as far as all can show?
Is the night so midnight blue?

Is the night a murky green,
thick and hazy,
clouding over all reality,
breathing heavy spoiled stanch
like rotted flesh long-ready for burial
in earthen sanctuary,
where moss-covered dreams
and silenced screams
like dried up streams
are not heard or felt, nor missed nor mourned?
Is night the green of slime
where solid footing isn't found,
where ebb and flow lamenting sound,
too thick to mold the slightest wave,
a sickly green, an open grave?
Is night a murky green?

Or is the night a bloody red,
screaming loud of murd'rous dread,
great chanting of revolt,
a severing sword which slices heart,
not in one quick and mighty dart,
but hour by hour grinding low?
Is night dripping crucible of beat
stretched open, barred in wrenching heat
of burning crimson,
a trickling, pulsing scarlet pain
mapping its indel'ble stain
on a bleeding soul
which never could again be whole?
Is the night a bloody red?

Is the night a purple deep,
a royal cloak of deathly sleep
from which there's no awakening,
a radiating passion of despair
wrought empty of all royal care,
deep violet yoke of burdened day,
which strapped and fastened tightly,
can't be striped away?
Is night an indigo wash upon the sky
wrenching hours of lonely cry,
like o'er-ripe grapes in scorch of sun
stomped flat, down-run
in paralyzing liquid sleep?
Is the night a purple deep?

Or is the night just graceful bow
of rain's delight 'gainst amber glow,
like teardrop's prism,
a glorious blend at setting sun
that breathes a timeless, lucid rest
into a wearied golden breast
that cannot lay its head more willingly?
Is the night a pearly stain
that sleeps in vain on vacant shell
'til morning rays in splendor tell
that night is but a brief delay,
that color soon will bend and shine its ray,
that dark of night precludes more radiant day?
Then night is but a rainbow's smile,
a grace of God, to stay awhile.
Is this the color of the night—
that which paints the dark to light?

Water Music

The sun is singing melody
    on river's flow
        that's dared to break
            from winter's dark and clamy grasp.
Graceful ripples resonate freedom chants
        from glassy channel
            of frozen silence.
Fragile prisms of melting crystals
    fight for one last pink or purple gasp
        before being swept up and away
            in symphony of blended, bluish silver.

Ancient iron bridge,
    burnished orange and brown with crusty rust,
        securely, bravely crosses cleft
            of age-old millstream basin,
    strengthening, resounding,
        in timeless, low, deep-dark, mysterious silence.

Railroad ties,
    one, then another, still yet another,
            resting tranquilly,
        aged, cracked,
            licked wet by melting frozenness,
A wooden xylophone
    stretched above a sparkling sea of glass,
        reverberating tones of otherness—
            other worlds, other times,
                other ways.

Golden rays
    in milky rainbows from above,
        set off electrifying sparks of energy
    waiting, pausing,
        for conductor's cordial cue.

In dome of magical, musical silence—
        liquid scene of peaceful mystery,
            here I am.
        the key wound, my footsteps on the bars,
        awaiting the moment,
            to set in motion
        the tune of God's own heavenly orchestration.

Train In The Night

A train is passing in the night.
On its rumbling rails it follows its flight,
traversing nearby bridge o'er city street.
Each car hammers its blows in repetitious fanfare
as earth with steel meet
with rhythmic thudding.
Once and again and again.
One and another and another,
like a procession of angry, weathered, disposable beasts
following their master in unquestioning peace.

Between the methodical thuddings
whispers a melodious murmur
lulling in beckoning beat.
And within me, deep desire yearns to rise
from restless and encumbered sleep,
this stationary cipher in which I am entrapped,
to coalesce
with rolling, rusting, steel parade of coffins
recording moments of the night,
that I, too, may disappear from sight
into silenced seconds that promise restful light.

Or have I already laid that which was me,
piece by piece by nauseous piece,
in every beastly, rumbling crease
of moving metal,
sold and shipped like cheapened meat,
made rancid in intolerable heat,
with maggots crawling in decay, and beat,
who, with hushed weep, in restless anguish
searches deep within myself
the scattered pieces there to keep?

Or is it I who screams in terror in the night
as car on car take endless flight,
because it's I who lie upon the track
as steel on steel with force attack?
I, knifed and shredded, butchered
lack
even the voice
to counterattack.

A train is passing in the night,
In mysterious allurement, I yearn to join flight.

Struggle Of Triumph
Tribute to Sandy

I called to God, I cursed Him out,
    He let me rave, He let me shout.

I told God it's not fair or right,
    That He should turn my "day" to "night."

I crumbled senseless in my waste,
    And begged this cup I might not taste.

I cried to God to leave, to go,
    How could He let me suffer so?

God came to me and held me tight,
    He took my heart and soothed my fright.

God wrapped His loving arms around,
    And cradled me without a sound.

God put His strength within my soul,
    He gave me peace and made me whole.

God spoke to me, called out my name,
    And ask, "Dear child, why cry in vain?"

And then I knew in this, in all,
    God loves me so, I'll never fall.

With blessed assurance, holy light,
    God turns my dark world back to bright.

And with God's strength from Heaven above,
    I walk in faith, and hope, and love.

There To Here

In Memory of my Dad

It was so brief from there to here,
    Like seconds on a clock,
        Like ray of sun amidst the clouds,
        Like stroll along a dock.

It was so still form there to here,
    Like turning of a leaf,
        Like silent song of butterflies,
        Like wave on far 'way reef.

It was so pure from there to here,
    Like puff within a cloud,
        Like ivory of a piano key,
        Like whisper spoke aloud.

It was so small from there to here,
    Like blossoms 'neath a tree,
        Like earthworm breaking through the ground,
        Like opening for a key.

It was so sweet from there to here,
    Like honey in a comb,
        Like nectar of a wildflower,
        Like house become a home.

It was so fine from there to here,
    Like hairs upon a head,
        Like velvet knap of finest robe,
    Like feathers of a bed.

It was so smooth from there to here,
　　Like mellow touch of wine,
　　　　Like carpet of a grassy lawn,
　　　　　　Like curious twist of vine.

It was so short from there to here,
　　Like blinking of an eye,
　　　　Like sand within an hourglass,
　　　　　　Like kiss without good-bye.

I grasp the small, the sweet, the short,
　　The brief I hold until…
　　　　Along with fine, and smooth, and pure,
　　　　　　I find you with me still.

The Sea

Thalassa—Greek word for "sea"

Thalassa, Thalassa, great breath of the sea,
    Why do you whisper and beckon to me?
  Why do you call in a silence like night,
  You moan in your ebbing in a groaning delight?
  Why call you, why call you,
     To me in my fright?

I sense that a treasure you hold in your deep,
  A rich gift, most rare, in foreboding you keep,
   Why pause I, why pause I,
     From most welcomed sleep?

I gaze on the glisten of surface' soft glow,
  As stars reach from heaven and touch you below,
   You answer, you answer,
     In soft tones, and low.

Below in the chasm, hear echoes of shell,
  They break forth in ripple, a story to tell,
   What say you, what say you,
     From deep in your well.

Your lucid, long arms reach out forth, then pull back,
  Then on forth again, and soon back to retrack,
   They pull me, they pull me,
     With their power attack.

You inhale slowly, so slowly, then out,
  In your whispering silence, I gasp in your shout,
   All glory, all glory,
     Your voice breathes devout.

The wavelet's delight and the breaker's loud roar,
The fish down below, above eagles that soar,
We praise Him, we praise Him,
It echoes on shore!

I stand on the edge as sea offers me lease,
To what'er you possess that might grant to me peace,
I breathe in, I breathe in,
A most holy release.

Thalassa, Thalassa, great breath of the sea,
Your whispering murmurs, in grace, set me free.

Stone From The Sea

A stone from the sea
was once given to me,
polished smooth and fine
by the lap of the waves
that curled its line
through oceans of days,
that wore on its edges
that pulled at its core
'til the stripes of its history
told all the more
of the days of the earth
spread out of God's store.

I held onto it tight,
the cold in my hand,
my fingers encircling it,
band upon band.
I bore its full weight,
first left and then right,
and felt of its shiver
in the dark of the night.

Solid and steady
it breathed in my palm
'til I thought that I heard,
in the veil of calm,
the swish of the waves
as they beat on the sand
of a shore
in a distant and faraway land
that I only could know of,
the shape only guess,
by the sound and the whisper
in my own mind's caress
of this piece of eternity,
this stone from the sea,
the weight of this gift
which was given to me.

Exile

What is this exile
in which I tarry?

Is it an exile
of a body
that has no home
in a world of things
no longer having meaning,
where those very things
which should bring joy
are the burdens
weighing as heavy, rock-hard stone
upon a pair of shoulders
no longer able
to bear the burden
of the load?

Is it an exile
of a heart
resting uneasily
in the hollow, lonely
cavity of chest
it must, for now,
call home,
where love is fleeting memory
intangible, unreachable "uncaring"
which seeps in sieve-like transience
and unending, earthly meaninglessness.

Is it an exile
of a spirit
bound tightly to its mortality,
piled high in mound
of immovable, impenetrable murkiness,
where sweeps of sunshine
or billowing puffs of cloud
are blotted out
in ominous, foggy encirclement,
where "yearning" aches its emptiness
in silent spaces
no waft of breeze
can scatter
from its path.

Or, is it an exile
of a soul
screaming in desolation
in unending trilogies
of longing desperation,
where empty moments
of empty hours
of empty days
stagnate in the immobility
of bleeding breaths,
whimpering in inaudible tones
of unending nothingness?

Oh, to be held—
only to be held again
in the comforting arms
of the Father,
only to be held again,
to be 'home" again.

Exile, exile,
Father,
why must I walk
in exile
when I'm ready
to come home.

She And I

Sometimes when I'm lonely,
I go looking for her,
at the lake,
by the road ditch,
try to catch a glimpse of her,
a reflection in the river dark as ebony.
Can't find her!
I look down again
and there she is,
translucent in an oozing mirror
that flows of blood—
or is it blackness?

She is the question
that begs for an answer,
a flow that chides me
come and follow.
I grasp her fluid hand.

Sometimes we start climbing.
Her weight pulls me from behind.
She is so heavy,
a weight like iron,
a rusting, rotting relic of the past,
no longer belonging to me,
but binding me in memory just the same.

Sometimes she comes to me.
Invisible
she lures me back,
not touching me at all.
Together we disappear
to where it's safe,
where all the pain doesn't hurt anymore,
where she and I are one.
And I become transparent too,
suspended into nothingness,
bound by nothingness.

And we escape together
to fly the blue
like geese flying southward
in perfect formation
to where there is warmth.
She the question,
I the answer.
Reunited. Sentenced!

Candlesticks On The Lake

As evening gently melts the western sun,
its blanket falls heavily o'er the lake.
Darkness cradles the glimmering waters
while walkway lamplights fall
as burning candlesticks on a shimmering sea.
A blue moon slithers mosaic wedges of glass,
mirror to mirror,
shore to shore,
painting the landscape
with a flickering presence—
the holy abode of the grace of God.

Prairie Child

The silent breeze curls around me
and sends the prairie grasses swaying
in a steady, rhythmic motion—
breathing…
back and forth, in and out,
the breath of God
visible in earthly matter.

Mesmerized,
I stand silent
feeling the ebb and flow
also in myself.

Soaring into the beckoning breeze
like a wild bird
flung loose from its cage,
I dance gracefully, silently—wildly
in the freedom of the moment,
transported willingly heavenward.

A raven, a butterfly, an angel,
I disappear
into the ocean of blue canvas and billowy cloud.

Prayer Without Words

O God,
How I need to talk to you,

But, alas,
the words are fettered in my soul,
and
screaming sentences lay silenced
in a prison of despair.

In trails of tears
that etch upon my cheek,
and in the burdened breaths
emitting from my depths,
the wordless pleas are spoken.

Thank you, God,
for listening to my cries
and for hearing words
in silent sighs.

Amen

Vine Prayer

The silvery, brown stems
slither their way along
    the gray matrix of fence wire,
clinging precariously to sidewalls
    of cool, smooth cement,
creeping silently, insidiously
    around window frame and pane,
grasping hungrily
    at surrounding plant life,
        which sleeps thirstily
        in late August sun.

Almost hidden from view
tiny, naked tendrils
curve over and around
    shoots, and stems, and crevices,
clinging hopefully
for support, for growth, for life.

You, dear Jesus, the vine
    that would never give up the possibility
    of nourishing lifeblood
    to the drying spirit
    that cannot even be named a branch.
You the crisscrossed maze
    that cradles the aching heart.
You the tendril that would hold on, grasp tight
    the withering shoot,
        keeping it from stumping into silence.

Wrap your tendrils round about me now
    that I may feed on your unending giving,
    that I may rest in your undying love,
    that I may sprout and grow
        carried within the very breath of God.

Sending Psalm

A thousand, million, mighty stars
    shine out of the billowy heavens
        in the brightness of the day.
And I am crushed by the weight
    of their deep, blue brilliance
        saturating the core of my being.
They scream the sheer silence
    of a holiness and graciousness
    my meager mind can but begin
        to understand.

Your breathing, God,
    is in the gentle breeze
    that quivers the downy hairs
        upon my arms,
    yet tears me from my moorings,
        like a tired boat on the open sea.

I sense your hand reaching out
    to cup me up in gentleness.
Then you set me forth in a blazing chariot,
        like a voice crying in the wilderness.
And I am compelled
    to enter the fiery furnace of your beckoning,
  not to leave the world,
    which your power created with a spoken word,
        but to enter it
        in all its depth and intensity.

Why, God?
I ask, why am I to be the chosen handmaiden
    to bear your love
    to a callus, disregarding, unforgiving humanity?

The depth of the hurt of the ages
    whispers in the flickering flame
        of the eternal candle
        on your altar's mantle.
And, as I kneel before your awesome throne,
    every pore of my being
        cries in a childlike, responsive refrain:
Here I am, Lord God. Send me, send me.

Later Poems . . .

A Pastor's Doubt

She lay there…
as still as the seconds before a storm strikes,
her wrought frame heavy in the bedclothes,
her paper-thin cheek skin drawn taut and hollow,
her searching eyes sunken into their blue-green sockets,
her speckled, parchment hand trembling and ashen gray,
opening and closing, opening and closing,
as I gently stroked her cool, scarred arm.

She was in her dying moments.
She, and everyone else in the room, knew it.
I knew it—I, her pastor, her guide,
her trusted partner on this unknown journey into death.

As I smoothed the age-worn skin of her forearm,
I spoke gently, calmly, in whispered tones,
sounding seasonedly sure of the words
spilling from my hiddenly-trembling lips,
"In my Father's house, there are many dwelling places."
"There is a place for you, Edythe," I assured her.
"Your husband and your son are waiting
with outstretched, welcoming arms."
Her searching eyes looked skyward,
her hand relaxed,
and with a last, insignificant breath,
she left us.

Am I so sure of my words these days
as I look up to the heavens
and let the rain pelt down my hair and face?
As the white-gray gull swoops scoldingly over the lake?
As the angry, midnight-blue waves
eat away at a forgotten sandcastle on the shore?

My chest is filled with panic.
The ache bolts like lightening through my body,
my heart pounds out loud.
The flash of an instant passes.
But, in that time-torn second,
it is there, sure and certain—
a pastor's doubt.

Faltering Faith

When I get weighed down
by strict rules, heavy creeds,
and the righteous hierarchy of religion,
and I feel my faith falter,
I go to where the water spills loosely over the rocks,
where the cool, fir-green trees stand majestic
against the piercing, blue sky,
where the rainbows of birds and butterflies
take wing carelessly and unconstrained over the flowered cavern.
There I feel you once again, God,
mighty and powerful and loving altogether.
There all you ask of me is "me,"
just as I am, just who I am.
There my spirit is re-birthed
and I am free to love you once again.

You Met Me There

Most unexpectedly,
You met me there.

Up the winding ribbon of road,
Atop the mellow hillside,
In the white-paneled church,
Sitting silently on a bed of snow,
You met me.

I entered the Sanctuary—
Your sanctuary—
Having long given in
To the painful emptiness
Of Your lacking presence.

Yet, most unexpectedly,
You met me there,
Not in any words of incantation, prayers, or spoken message,
And not in traditions
White-robed in candlelight and silver vessels.

You met me in the sway of melody
Flowing from the pipe-crowned organ.
You met me in the gentle brush of breeze
From swirling fan blades high above.
You met me in the rainbow-paletted lightbeams
Filtering the sleepy, December sunshine
Into the cavernous space of worship.

And You did more than meet me there.
You swaddled and nestled me,
A newborn baby
United once again with its nursing mother.
You nudged me,
A wandering and wayward bird,
And lifted me back
Into a path of flight-filled freedom.
You whispered LOVE into my ear
And pressed me with your Spirit.

Now I journey on in peace,
Filled, fulfilled, and blessed,
Just because, dear God,
You met me there.

Willow, Why Are You Weeping?

Willow, why are you weeping?
Do you weep
because your neighbor, the ash
stands dun and dried
against the forceful, November wind,
which sways
your rust-bronzed spindles
but rips the ash's delicate foliage
from her heart?

Or do you weep
because the leafy maple's attire
curls away from your side,
wild winds sending the frost-bit leaves
rolling tumultuously
down the glaze-coated street,
leaving you
forlornly brown and friendless?

Do you weep
because the vari-colored bloom-field
beneath your feet
has crumbled into nothingness,
replaced by sordid, black patchiness?
And the duck platoon
that paddled the glassy pond,
crowded out by an icy mirror,
has abandoned you
for warmer moorings?

Once there was a woman
who sought the tomb
of her Master,
who had been ripped from life
on the cross
in the cold and the wind and the storm,
only to meet Him, unsuspecting, as the gardener.
"Woman, why are you weeping?"—
his words to her.
"They have taken my Lord,
and I do not know where they have laid Him."
she replied.
He again—"The **SON** has risen!
Weep no more.
Let joy and hope replace your sadness
for out of death comes life!
That's the way it is with God.
It is God's promise!"

Willow, as the **SON** has risen,
your **SUN** will also rise,
and its warmth will lift your spirits
out of the frozen mire.
Your tawny fronds
will burst triumphant
as tender, green tendrils
wafting in the balmy breeze.
The maple, the ash, and
the colorful blooms in your foot-space
will once again adorn you
side to side.

Your paddling companions
will rejoin the party, frolicking
as the soothing springtime
hastens in.

So Willow,
weep no more.
Let joy and hope replace your sadness
for out of death comes life!
It is that way with God.
It is God's promise!
Alleluia. Amen.

Begging Woman

There she stood,
one foot on the dull, concrete curb,
the other in the crew-cut, shorn grass,
rusty-orange backpack beside her
where seeded blades waved in the wind.
Her stern, but longing,
sun-baked face searching.
A brown, corrugated sign
in her wrinkled fingers—
"homeless and hungry
    please help
    GOD bless
    thank you"
printed in black crayon.

Stuck at the traffic light
I looked over at her,
quickly turning away
when she returned the favor—
I did not want her eyes to meet mine,
struggling with guilt as I was.
Should I or shouldn't I help her?

Thirteen dollars and some odd cents
in the purse beside me on the seat,
supposed to last through the weekend—
today only Thursday.
"Used" before,
I had reasoned not to let it happen again.
Yet her presence plagued me.

When you did not do it to the least of these,
you did not do it to me."
Did I see Jesus in her face?
I glanced and looked away again—
remembering
I had been so close to being her—
so close myself when out of work.

Yet, I saw her blue, denim jeans
not ragged,
her navy-trimmed, yellow T-shirt
faded but clean,
her amber tendrils nearly braided behind her head.
Should I or shouldn't I help her?
"When you did not do it to the least of these,
you did not do it to me."
Jesus' words again.

Am I not like her, God,
when I come before you,
begging for mercy—
or for whatever else you might offer?
Oh, how I am hungry for your love,
not truly at home in this world,
my home away from home.
Am I not like her, God?

"When you did not do it to the least of these,
you did not do it to me," Jesus' words.
But also Jesus' words—
"You will always have the poor with you,"
I recall.
Is it okay for me to leave her there?

The traffic light greened.
Pushed forward
by the parade of vehicles behind me,
I drove on, ridden with guilt
but also relief—
relief to put space between us.
I did not look back to see if others stopped.

God, I hope you will forgive me
if, selfishly, I erred this day.

The Voice

The wind was rushing
like slivers
through the rustling, leaf-ripened branches.
Deep, penetrating sun-fingers
seared the earth-warmed grasses.
There was an insignificant whistling
through softened reeds,
and a blazing
that had no crackling tongue-flames.

The rush of the wind
said nothing,
neither did the sun's burning.
But in their silence,
there was something
smaller than a flicker,
a barely audible whisper.

The ancient Hebrew tradition
uttered in memorized, oral tone...
God is not in the wind,
not in the fire,
but in the still, small voice.

In that void between wind and flame,
rush and burning,
breath and breath again,
I heard it—the voice,
God's voice.

Nearly silent, barely perceptible,
nothing really to hear at all,
like an exhalation,
yet penetrating.
Except for an inner knowing,
I would not have even noticed.
Yet, in that life-changing
moment of recognition,
I knew with humble certainty
that my life would never be the same.

Home In God's Arms
A Love Poem to God

When I feel alone, God,
you are there,
there to reach out to me,
and to wait for me
to reach my hand back,
to grasp yours
and hang on.
You draw me to yourself.
I, relieved to be found,
fall into your arms,
lay my head on your shoulder,
and know I am home,
safe and warm and loved
again.

Pigeons On The Marquee

An Observation

I wait on the sidewalk
for the grinding halt
of the city bus,
the telltale smell of diesel fuel
filling the air.

Above me,
to my surprise,
a flock of blue-gray pigeons,
huddled together against the wind,
along the edge of the theatre marquee,
shivering,
watching taxis and buses go by,
shoppers down below,
waiting for some morsel of goodness
left for grabbing in the cold
to drop from careless hands.

Don't you know, dear birds,
your home is on the farm
resting on the solid beams
of the haymow,
safe and warm,
a feast of freshly-milled deliciousness
waiting down below?

I board the bus
and leave them there,
sad, forlorn, and hungry.
After all,
this is the city,
the place they know as home.
Who am I to decide where they belong?

The Road Rose Up

The scorching sun had beaten down maliciously
on the gray-black, tarred street,
hour on hour of parched heat,
skies a bright, white light.

Out of nowhere
an angry, black cloud rushed in
covering the heavens with darkness.
Pelting rain blew horizontally
across the thirsty ground.
As quickly as it began, it was over.

Vapor, mist-like clouds
began to rise from the wet, hot roadbed,
first here, then there
until at last I was driving through a cloud—
or had I been transported into the heavens,
gentle, billowing moisture surrounding me.

"God, how beautiful is your creation,
how wonderful your works in all the earth!
Who am I that I should be worthy of them?"

Looking up I saw a pastel rainbow
stretching across the now blue sky,
gentle color as far as my eyes could see.
My journey truly blessed!

Yet She Was My Mother

Her final words to me—
"Now who are you?"
I winced at bit
to hear them so directly,
no longer recognized
by the one who gave me birth.

Her words finally confirmed
the abandonment
I had learned to live with.
Fruit of her womb,
flesh of her flesh,
I had never been,
nor could I be
the child she'd set her mind on.

She wanted children
to be in the spotlight,
to steal the show,
to win her acclaim,
to be, not just "good" but "great!"
I'd spent my life
trying to be "good enough."
Simply sharing heredity was not
reason sufficient to bind us.

Now we were down
to the final good-byes.
A steel-bronzed casket
in a white-clapboard church.
A few gray-haired, cane-bearing mourners—
ones who could remember her.
I had no words, no tears.
Relief filled all the empty spaces
as the organ hymn,
meant to honor and comfort,
bounced around my head
like some strange, rhythmic waltz.

We buried her there,
on the windswept, snow-blanketed prairie,
the bleak, sodden, November air
lapping at our faces.
Quiet and shy, withdrawn and deep,
the person I had always been
relinquished any hope
that one day she might know me as I was—
and love me.

How fitting,
how appropriate, her words—
"Now who are you?"—
for she will never know.
However, somewhere deep inside me,
there is an empty hole
where a little one cries
to be understood and loved,
and finally to be "good enough."
For, despite it all,
yet she was my mother.

Just Yesterday
A Tribute

"The generations rise and fall before you, O God."

I let my heavy eyelids fall closed
and, rushing into the momentary darkness,
there comes a flood of brilliance
like a moving picture show
of the "mothers" and "fathers" of my childhood days.

They are smiling and laughing,
and scolding and guiding,
wiping noses and washing faces,
bandaging knees and icing bruises,
wearing baggy denim overalls
with rolled-sleeve, red and blue, plaid shirts,
floral housedresses with flour-sack, home-sewn aprons,
helping a child swing a heavy wooden bat
or manage a food-filled, flowered, metal tray
along with an icy glass of cool, red sweetness.
They are visiting, and telling stories, and sharing news—
these "mothers" and "fathers" of mine.
I see it all
as if it were just yesterday.

These "mothers" and "fathers" of mine—
they were the mothers and fathers
of my "brothers" and "sisters"—
those with whom I grew up
closer than blood relatives,
sharing day in and day out and quiet Sunday afternoons
in the cool shadows of a corn crib playhouse,
or hiding in a pile of sunflower-colored straw bales
inside a musty, cobwebbed-filled cattle barn,
or playing "spoons" 'til our knuckles were bleeding
and, laughing so hard, we thought our sides would burst

while krispy bars were being stirred in an old, gray kettle,
and the smell of tuna fish and fresh bread
wafted from the yellow-curtained kitchen.

We, who played, bore babies of our own,
and these "mothers" and "fathers" of mine
mothered and fathered both us and our offspring.
We were so busy, we didn't notice
they were playing less and sitting more,
growing more round or more crooked with time.
We brought the food, and washed the dishes,
and cleaned the messes, and wiped the faces.
But they were there right alongside us,
lending a helping hand when needed,
cheering us and our children on,
'til golden anniversaries passed them by,
and the sun began to set on their earthbound years,
and, in turn, on ours with them.
Still, I see them all,
as if it were just yesterday.

Now we, the children, bound by common time and place,
are grandparenting our children's children.
Time has scattered us like confetti in the breeze—
these "brothers" and "sisters" of mine and me.
My "mothers" and "fathers" are all but gone,
most steeled and sealed,
resting under green grass blankets,
heavy, cast markers bearing their names
resting at their heads.
Yet, they live on—
these "mothers" and "fathers" of mine.

Unknowingly and innocently, from the time I can remember,
I watched the days of their lives tick by.
I saw them live and love and laugh,
and age,
and, in time, die.
It all happened in the blink of an eye.
In a breath of air, they walked the earth
and left their mark for me to wear—forever.
I close my eyes, and they are here again,
always holding, always guiding, always loving.

"For all the saints, who from their labors rest..."
plays its melody in recesses in my memory.
Peacefulness attends my spirit.
I close my eyes, and I see it all again,
as if it were just yesterday.

Rain In The Night

In the sleepy hours of the night,
windows wide open
to the warmth of the season,
I lie awake
listening to the rain
beating the pavement.
It is a lulling sound,
like a melody in the background
broken up
by the occasional crescendo and decrescendo
of car tires on the watery pavement.
A shrill, but muted siren
sounds in the distance
adding flavor to the night's music.
The smell of fresh-cut grass
wafts its greenness
into my dark cocoon of room.
Curled in the covers,
I smell sweetness.
I breathe in a long, satisfying breath.
Aromatic water music!
My peaceful heart sings its joy.
What a gift, God.
What a gift!

Spirits Rising

Tribute to the victims of the 35-W bridge collapse
Minneapolis, Minnesota
August 1, 2007

There are spirits rising,
I feel them.

Gazing at the sight
of the bridge's falling,
I felt them,
wreckage in the river,
iron beams bent
like twist ties,
cars haphazardly
scattered to broken concrete,
half in the river,
half above,
bodies screaming
from beneath the water.

Today a new bridge,
bravely strong,
concrete pillars
on either end
waving to the sun.
Spirits still rising,
hovering against the wind,
basking in the warmth,
spirits of moms and dads and grandparents,
young women and young men,
workers of the day,
a child… an unborn baby.

You are not forgotten, dear ones,
you, who died so unexpectedly
that brilliant August afternoon.
You are not forgotten.
Prayers now still rising
that you are safely in God's care.

Dancing Leaves

"So do not worry about tomorrow
for tomorrow will bring worries of its own."

The spiced-crimson leaves
of the maple tree
smile with their lacy edges
at the October sunshine,
dancing in the gentle breeze of autumn,
fluttering down
across the sun-dried, velvet blanket
of shorn grasses
in a jolly promenade.

Don't they know
they will soon crisp into nothingness,
leaving naked, frozen branches,
sullen and still,
to face the brisk November wind?

Dance, my pretty leaves, dance!
Frolic in the wind.
Worry about tomorrow's shortening days
when they whisk bitterly in!

Season's Changing

The snowflakes rest,
a fine, white layer
like tissue paper
coating the peaked roofs,
billowing pillars
of gray-white smoke
floating from chimneys
into the frigid November air.

Winter's setting in,
saying goodbye
to the brown, fall crispness,
saying goodbye
to the brilliant sun
coloring orange and yellow
on the piles of leaves
still sleeping in heaps
along winding boulevards.

Standing atop
a weary, rusted bridge,
I turn to face
the brisk, northwesterly wind,
drawing a deep breath,
walking on
into the wintery future of barrenness
with the only thing
I have to give it,
hope for a brighter tomorrow.

Psalm Of Joy

Dear God, you are so near to me,
I can sense you surrounding me,
filling me up within.

With you, I am bathed
in the sunshine and warmth
of a rainbow of springtime flowers
reaching,
with hands outstretched,
up to the heavens,
smiling at the sunrays.

I am immersed in the gentle breeze
waffling its way around
rocks and crooks
as it meanders
in your sea of love.

I can hold out my palms,
and tender raindrops
cast from your mighty hands
roll over me as a protective shield.

I breathe in the gift
of your exhaled whispers
like delicate, but powerful, waves
lapping the nearby shore.

I am strengthened
as I am surrounded and held,
filled and sustained
by the peaceful joy, Dear God,
of your abiding presence.

O God, You Are My God

A Psalm of Praise

O God, you are my God,
　　my joy in all the earth.

The darkness cannot hide your face from me,
　　evil cannot push you far away.
Your Spirit is my ever-present friend,
　　your breath within my breath.

When I rise, I rise to you,
　　when I walk, I walk for you.
Your love is in my arms to share,
　　your voice is given voice through me.

O God, you are my God,
　　my joy in all the earth.

My Trinity
A Tribute to the Church of my Birth

In my thoughts
I walk through
the little, white, clapboard church,
standing so lonely
out on the prairie,
the church
of every important occasion
since my birth,
baptisms and communions,
confirmations and weddings,
funerals—
the saying goodbye
to my great-grandparents,
grandparents,
parents,
now resting with their backs
to the prairie winds,
whisper quiet and motionless.

I am taken
by the pure simplicity
of it all.

This place,
the center of my childhood universe,
now sleepy and quiet…
… I fear slowly dying also.
"For everything there is a season,"
The season of Trinity, my Trinity,
gradually coming to a close.
I am so fortunate to have had you,
little church,
as I grew into personhood,
shaped by the faith,
by the love
of the fathers and mothers before me.

How can something so insignificant
have such a lifetime impact
on my life,
on my faith?

Holy is your name, dear church,
Holy is your name.

Busy Hands Now Still
Tribute to Sadie

As she lay on her final resting bed,
ivory crepe surrounding her
like a puffy cloud tinged with sunshine,
her hands, always busy,
now lie still,
folded mortician-style
across her lifeless body,
brown-speckled,
skin as thin as parchment paper,
showing the aging
her ninety-seven years of life
have given her.

First time I've ever seen those hands
not moving.
They had always been busy
caring, and sharing, and doing.
With her hands
she showed me what life is all about.
With an ever-ready smile,
she served love
through every homemade, Swedish meatball,
every piece of rich, moist dessert—
through every genuine hug!
Her hands always busy,
this final rest is much deserved.

"Well done, good and faithful servant."
I say, "Well done, good friend!"
May you rest safely in God's arms.

Sunflower Time

*"To everything there is a season
and a time for every purpose under heaven."*

The late August sun
yawns sleepy, golden rays
across the cloudless azure sky,
stretching the earth's expanse
with serene peacefulness.

Ripe, resplendent sunflowers
full in season, straight and tall,
with deep, velvety, earth-toned centers
lift their plated heads to the heavens
or bow their full-seeded bowls to the earth.

It is late summer…
in my life also,
aging with years,
not yet old, just "older,"
straight and tall with experience,
full and rich with thoughts,
deep and heavy with wisdom—
a field of flaxen grain ready for gleaning,
a willingness to share
what talent and knowledge alone cannot yield.

My arms are spread
to the world now,
a basket, fine woven and flared,
ready to be harvested—
to be emptied,
to be fruitful.
Myself a bouquet
of vibrant yellow petals
overflowing with fragrance,
ready to infuse,
to hold life in its caress.

Simple Thought

I rode
The merry-go-round of life
'til the strife
laid me bare.
From there
I learned
to trust you, God,
to lay my life
your way,
to let your guide
lead my stride
each and every day.

Melting Snow

A Poem of Adoration

After the bitter cold,
the snow softens to new warmth.
The melting ice
splatters
on the smooth cement below,
awakening into water
and puddling at my feet.

So my soul awakens
to the warmth
of your presence, God,
leaving the frozen mire
of this world's tireless demands,
and flowing
with reckless abandon,
to puddle at your feet,
there to worship and adore you,
the Source of my being,
my Lord, my Master,
and my eternal Friend.

Voice Crying In The Wilderness

Lord God,
I am a voice
crying in the wilderness,
surrounded by the strife
of suffering people
trying to have a life
in a world of callous disregard.

I sense the pain
of all the living souls
seeking respite from the cold
in the frigidness of winter
or in the winter of their lives.

I hear the heartache
of the young woman
who cannot bear a child,
of the old man
whom no one visits
for whom no one cares.

I feel the distress
of the worker
inundated with the anger
of his supervisor,
of the child
who has no bed of his own
in the shelter
his family now calls home.

I crumble to the fear
provoked by terrorists
who would harm innocent people,
murdering without remorse
in your name,
God,
in your name.

I am a voice
crying in the wilderness.
Hear my cries, Lord God.
Hear,
and come near.

Whispering God Prayer

Whispering God,
you who breathed in me
the breath of life
and set me on your path,
intoxicate me with your love,
that I may hear your voice
above the cacophony of noise
that fills this world
with all the sounds
that would lead me astray.

Carry me
gently in your arms,
that my feet may not wander
from your way,
that my words and my actions
may emanate your will
towards all creation.

Let me rest in your bosom,
safe and warm and cradled,
that I may be revived
for this journey of life
given me new each morning,
energized by the all-encompassing power
of your eternal presence.

And, at my journey's end,
envelop me in your kingdom
where I will sleep
in the presence of angels,
songs filling my heart,
finally fulfilled and reunited
with you,
my eternal source,
my peace, my joy, my love.
Amen.

Angels Song

There were voices
singing in the darkness,
sweet melody,
graceful song,
like a lullaby in my soul.

It felt like butterflies dancing
in an immense chasm,
and it lifted me gently
out of the dark void,
the inbetween of death and life,
from the place of waiting to live
while wanting to die.

In the song was a ray of assurance,
tender, yet steady and unquivering,
and a flowing of movement
from stagnancy to vitality.
My breath quickened to the harmony.

As my spirit joined the chorus,
I was lifted
by the soft, melodious stanzas,
for, into the depths of my heart,
the angels sang hope.

A Dream

I dreamed about you last night,
you, and you, and you, and you,
all of you
just who you were,
who you've been in my life,
but all together
in one story, in one dream.

How glad I was to see you again,
to hear your voices,
to know you once more.

I woke up full of longing
to have you in my story now,
each in your own way...
your smiles, your laughter,
your concern, your love.
your memory alive in my mind.

Thank you, God,
for how dreams and loved ones
come together
in stories
to cherish and remember.

Imminent Birth

To my unborn grandchild

Her usually long, lean body
has grown rotund
through time,
belly protruding
for the world to see
her personal experience
of expectant motherhood,
you within her.

Through the months and weeks,
and now, days and hours,
she has been co-creating
you with God,
a tiny human form
genetically transmitting
the hopes and dreams
of a new generation
into time and space.

Holy moments spent,
her breathing grows heavy,
her tired back screams rest,
beads of sweat
moisten her tawny locks.
With the might of her muscles
you will emerge from your dark, molten home
into this cold expanse of universe.
You will gasp as God breathes into you
the breath of life,
and you will exhale
that first, fine cry,
your song announcing,
"I am here. I am here…
… I AM. I AM."

Living Bookends

The elderly woman
reached for the baby,
slowly, carefully
drawing the precious bundle
into her fragile, sweatered arms,
veined and shriveled hands
grasping the tiny, warm body
in a gentle caress.

She stroked the baby's back,
up and down,
again and again,
cupping her hands
over the downy crown,
a smile of pure pleasure
on the woman's wrinkled face,
plump wonder on the child.

For holy moments
time stood still,
the elderly woman
and the baby together,
living bookends
on the spectrum of life.

Love Pledge

**A Prayer
on the occasion of my daughter's wedding**

There they stood
in front of God's altar,
holding hands,
taking vows,
her in graceful, ivory lace,
him in black, tuxedoed splendor,
beautiful and elegant,
a picture from a magazine.

Many successes trailed behind them,
gifts and skills,
diplomas and degrees,
jobs and professions,
all fulfilling in themselves,
yet leaving an empty space
in each one's heart.

In each other
they found the puzzle piece
that had been missing,
companionship,
partnership,
and, finally, love,
pure and holy,
deep and abiding.

Asking God to walk
with them and beside them,
they vowed their love
to one another,
a sacred moment
blessed by God,
the parent of all marriages.

God, may you join them
on their journey
in all that lies ahead
that their walk
may be a blessing
and a fulfillment
of their dreams.

Value

In a world
where progress and success
are the measure of everything,
where do I stand?

I pass my days
spending hours
for the sake of my children
… and grandchildren,
in prayer and meditation,
listening to song…
writing, painting, creating,
lending and ear to troubled souls.
Those are my days.
So where am I?

God, you are my source,
my foundation,
my life and my breath.
In you I live, God.
In you I love
and share that love
with those I meet.
You shape my "me."
You, my todays and tomorrows,
my forever.
You, my abiding joy.

To you I give myself—
just as I am,
and I trust you
to judge my value
with love.

In My Own Skin

I was like a puppy
with wrinkles and folds,
feet and hands too large.
But now, I have grown
into my own skin.

It's taken years and places,
time and spaces.
I've lived both there and here,
far and near.
I've given myself away
and taken myself back again.
I've run wolf-wild
and curled up kittenly soft.
I've become what other people wanted of me,
but, in the end, have saved myself,
afraid I would disappear.

I've held and hugged
and spread my arms to the breeze,
open and ready
to grow more knowledgeable—
and more kind.
Leaves have both greened and goldened
as I slowly and quietly—
or sometimes screaming and kicking—
evolved into being and understanding more wisely.

But I'm finally here,
no longer tripping on my own feet
or pulling my hand-skin away
from my fingertips.
I fit into me now,
comfortable—all of myself and in myself.

It is good to have arrived at this place
where I can reach up to the sun and smile.
Now I can flow like the wind
into an eternity of future,
free and untethered—
at last.

The Meshing

Some eighteen odd years ago
I left my home, my life,
cold, and dark, and empty
though it was,
me,
scattered in multi-layered directions,
broken, confused, alone, and lonely,
yet listening to a voice,
a voice of me, yet not my own.

Reluctant to return,
I found in all the new fulfillment,
in the re-creating of myself,
in the rebirth of springtime
following the sleet-cold frost of winter,
a certain emptiness in memory,
a disjointedness of being
that longed for continuity.

I'd left not knowing
who behind me
understood, cared, or supported.
I did not know if my confusion
melded into theirs.

Called back by duty,
to fulfill their need—
for a pastor to do services,
or maybe mine—
to connect the old with the new,
in apprehension I affirmed,
knowing walking into memories
as I was
might stir the spirit
triggering unhappiness—or fear.

Once there, the kettle stirred
and bubbled from within.
Could it be
these people of my birth,
of my former life,
accepted who now I was
when, so alone,
I took to the road
in search of myself?

I wear a baffled smile
pretending braveness, wholeness,
while my two worlds
stand in opposition
in which I belong to both
and, yet, not either.

Be patient with me, God,
A bridge's footings
may in time join land to land,
world to world
together.

Be patient with me, dear ones,
in your kindness,
my fellow travelers
on this journey
we call life,
for it will take some time
for me
to fuse the meshing into one,
and for it to web and grow.

Returning

I meandered
down the street
of the town
I left so long ago,
me,
harboring memories
somewhere deep inside
of its appearance,
and yet,
no longer belonging there.

Oh, it was familiar enough
from end to end
so that I knew my way,
knew which stores followed which,
though the storefronts
wore different faces—
different colors,
different names.

Familiar enough, this place,
and yet,
so very different,
Not something
I could put my finger on.

I still knew how many blocks
from the railroad tracks
to the highway,
though buildings were gone,
a parking lot resting
on one's grave.
The old, landmark, grain elevator
demolished,
torn down by progress,
silence echoing the memory
of where it used to live.

Things were
as they were supposed to be,

and yet, the town slept in a way
it hadn't before.
A vacuum had eaten up
the life
I used to know there.
And now I belonged,
and yet,
I didn't.

Shall I say good-bye
to the picture
in my mind
of this place
I once called home?
Shall I say good-bye
to memories
that both hold and haunt me?

Or,
shall I remember
that I, too, have changed,
have grown and matured,
that I'm the same,
yet different too,
and that "changing"
can be a gift—God's gift.
And, it can, in time, indeed, be good?

You Carry Me

O God, you carried me
through stormy skies and windy gales.
And I was able to walk on water
because you raised your arms beneath me
and drew me up from the well,
lifting me out of the tumultuous mire.

Even when my faith
flew away like the wind,
when doubt pelted me like hail,
when it seemed no one cared,
you were there,
trustworthy and true,
firm, and mighty, and powerful altogether.
You took me in your enormous embrace,
and I melted into the warmth of your bosom.
I let your footprints be my strength.

God, even now you carry me
when I feel weak,
no longer able to paint a smile on my face,
nor able to stand up straight and tall
with my head to the wind,
to put one foot before the next.

And when the firmaments of my life
rest in the peacefulness of daylight,
or rainbows appear out of nowhere
to illumine my path,
you are here to carry me,
still firm, and mighty, and powerful,
raining blessings on my heart.

God, even now I am carried forward
by your ever-present, all-encompassing love,
the soothing balm of your peacefulness
wrapping itself around my spirit.
Because you are here,
my breathing calms.
And I am able to continue as your messenger
because you are my beloved.
Through all joys and in all trials,
with you I live and love,
just because you carry me.

Happiness Crept In

Somewhere
between sadness and melancholy,
anxiety and night terrors,
happiness crept in,
insidious at first,
just a tingling of a feeling
I had not experienced
in a world of ages,
a song playing in the darkness,
a sonnet singing in the silence,
a smile on the heart
that permeated my soul,
my mind,
and finally,
swept out dancing on my lips.
There was a different hue in the air,
a brightness,
a radiance,
like a rainbow.
And a melody burst the skies
with abundant reverberation.
I sank to the sunshine's rays
and spent a tear
laughing at the joy of it,
for when I least expected
happiness crept in.